THE QUILTED Y·E·A·R

Imagine a **lively, whimsical quilt** that lets your eyes wander through a year-long panorama in a few pleasing moments. We've created a fanciful quilt in a **kaleidoscope of color** that celebrates the unfolding of the months, from January to December. This splendid quilt incorporates lots of techniques — quick-method piecing, template piecing, satin-stitched appliqué, paper piecing, and embroidery. Three-dimensional embellishments add to its interest and originality.

Enjoy creating two **wall hangings** using elements from the sampler: happy children in a row or bright baskets and flowers contrasted against a black background. A handsome wool felt **tote bag** is emblazoned with patriotic appliquéd designs. Intermediate to advanced quilters will discover a wealth of quilting pleasure in these heartfelt creations. There's a little of everything here … for everyone!

EDITORIAL STAFF

Vice President and Editor-in-Chief: Sandra Graham Case. *Executive Director of Publications:* Cheryl Nodine Gunnells. *Senior Publications Director:* Susan White Sullivan. *Leaflets Publications Director*: Mary Sullivan Hutcheson. *Editorial Director:* Susan Frantz Wiles. *Photography Director:* Karen Hall. *Art Operations Director:* Jeff Curtis. TECHNICAL — *Technical Editor:* Lisa Lancaster. *Technical Writer:* Frances Huddleston. EDITORIAL — *Associate Editor:* Steve Cooper. ART — *Art Publications Director:* Rhonda Shelby. *Art Imaging Director:* Mark Hawkins. *Art Category Manager:* Lora Puls. *Graphic Artists:* Laura Adkins and Jenny Dickerson. *Photostylist:* Janna Laughlin. *Publishing Systems Administrator:* Becky Riddle. *Publishing Systems Assistants:* Clint Hanson, John Rose, and Chris Wertenberger. DESIGN — *Designer:* Linda Tiano.

BUSINESS STAFF

Publisher: Rick Barton. *Vice President, Finance:* Tom Siebenmorgen. *Director of Corporate Planning and Development:* Laticia Dittrich. *Vice President, Retail Marketing:* Bob Humphrey. *Vice President, Sales:* Ray Shelgosh. *Vice President, National Accounts:* Pam Stebbins. *Director of Sales and Services:* Margaret Reinold. *Vice President, Operations:* Jim Dittrich. *Comptroller, Operations:* Rob Thieme. *Retail Customer Service Manager:* Stan Raynor. *Print Production Manager:* Fred F. Pruss.

Made in the United States of America

ISBN 1-57486-455-6

10 9 8 7 6 5 4 3 2 1

We wish to thank the excellent quilters who pieced, appliquéd, and embroidered the projects for this book: Larcie Burnett, Nelwyn Gray, and Glenda Taylor. We also thank Julie Schrader for her creative machine quilting.

TABLE of CONTENTS

SAMPLER QUILT

Finished Size: 55" x 67" (140 cm x 170 cm)

YARDAGE REQUIREMENTS

Yardage is based on 43"/44" (109 cm/112 cm) wide fabric. The Sampler Quilt is sewn in sections. Those sections are then assembled to make the quilt. This quilt is perfect for fabric scraps left over from other projects. However, if you choose to buy fabrics or feel that you don't have enough fabric in your collection, below is the **approximate** *total yardage you will need to complete all sections, as well as a complete list of supplies. Refer to* **Section Instructions**, *pages 8 – 83, for specific fabric and supply requirements.*

For sections:

$1^3/_8$ yds (1.3 m) of white solid fabric

$^3/_4$ yd (69 cm) of cream solid fabric

$^1/_8$ yd (11 cm) of black solid fabric

$2^1/_2$ yds (2.3 m) *total* of assorted cream and tan print fabrics

1 yd (91 cm) *total* of assorted red print fabrics

$1^1/_8$ yds (1 m) *total* of assorted green print fabrics

$1^1/_2$ yds (1.4 m) *total* of assorted blue print fabrics

$^3/_8$ yd (34 cm) *total* of assorted brown print fabrics

$^5/_8$ yd (57 cm) *total* of assorted gold print fabrics

$^1/_2$ yd (46 cm) *total* of assorted yellow print fabrics

$^1/_4$ yd (23 cm) *total* of assorted orange print fabrics

$^1/_4$ yd (23 cm) *total* of assorted pink print fabrics

Scrap of purple print fabric

$^1/_4$ yd (23 cm) of coral print fabric

$^1/_4$ yd (23 cm) of rust print fabric

$^1/_4$ yd (23 cm) of light pink solid fabric

For borders:

$^3/_8$ yd (34 cm) of white solid fabric

Approximately 1 yd (91 cm) *total* of print fabrics for pieced border

For finishing:

$4^5/_8$ yds (4.2 m) of fabric for backing and hanging sleeve

$^7/_8$ yd (80 cm) of fabric for binding

You will also need:

63" x 75" (160 cm x 191 cm) piece of batting

Transfer paper

Template plastic

Paper-backed fusible web

Stabilizer

Lightweight copy paper or white tissue paper

Embroidery floss: white, black, rust, gold, orange, pink, light green, medium green, and dark green

$9 – ^3/_8$" (9.5 mm) diameter buttons of assorted colors

White glass seed beads

$3 – ^5/_{16}$" (8 mm) black sew-on snaps

9" (23 cm) of $^1/_8$" (3 mm) wide white satin ribbon

Gold size #3 pearl cotton

CUTTING OUT THE BORDERS AND BINDING

Measurements include a $^1/_4$" seam allowance. Follow **Rotary Cutting**, *page 98, to cut pieces.*

From white solid fabric:

- Cut 6 **inner borders strips** $1^1/_2$"w.

From assorted print fabrics:

- Cut 4 **border squares** $4^1/_2$" x $4^1/_2$".

Reserve remaining assorted print fabrics for pieced borders.

From fabric for binding:

- Cut 1 **square for binding** 27" x 27".

MAKING THE SECTIONS

Individual section instructions are given on pages 8 – 83. Appliqué patterns are included for each section and are reversed. Pink lines on patterns indicate machine Satin Stitch details, grey lines indicate embroidery details, and dashed black lines indicate overlap. **Embroidery Stitches** *are given on pages 110 - 112.*

ASSEMBLING THE QUILT TOP

1. Sew **Sections 1 – 3** together as shown to make **Row 1**.

Row 1

2. Sew **Sections 4 – 7** together as shown to make **Row 2**.

Row 2

3. Sew **Sections 8 – 11** together as shown to make **Row 3**.

Row 3

4. Sew **Sections 12 – 14** together as shown to make **Row 4**.

Row 4

5. Sew **Rows 1 – 4** together to complete center section of quilt top.
6. Cut 2 **inner border strips** in half (at fold). Sew 1 half strip to each remaining **inner border strip** to make 4 **inner borders**.
7. Measure *length* across center of quilt top center. Trim 2 **inner borders** to determined measurement to make **side inner borders**. Attach **side inner borders** to quilt top center.
8. Measure *width* across center of quilt top center (including added borders). Trim remaining **inner borders** to determined measurement to make **top/bottom inner borders**. Attach **top/bottom inner borders** to quilt top center.
9. Measure *length* across center of quilt top. You will need to make 2 pieced **side outer borders** $4^1/_2$" x determined measurement. Using assorted prints, cut rectangles $4^1/_2$" x various lengths. Sew rectangles together to make 2 **side outer borders** $4^1/_2$" x determined measurement (ours measured $58^1/_2$").
10. Measure *width* across center of quilt top. In the same manner as **side outer borders**, piece 2 **top/bottom outer borders** $4^1/_2$" x determined measurement (ours measured $46^1/_2$").
11. Sew 1 **border square** to each end of **top** and **bottom** borders. Attach **side**, **top**, then **bottom outer borders** to quilt top.

6

COMPLETING THE QUILT

1. Follow **Quilting**, page 102, to mark, layer, and quilt. Our quilt is machine quilted.

2. Read **Making a Hanging Sleeve**, page 106, to add hanging sleeve to back of quilt.

3. Using **square for binding**, follow **Binding**, page 106, to bind quilt using $2^1/_2$"w bias binding with mitered corners.

Quilt Top Diagram

SECTION 1

Size (including seam allowance): $19^1/_2$" x $13^1/_2$"

YARDAGE REQUIREMENTS
BLOCK A
- 6" x 14" (15 cm x 36 cm) piece of red print fabric
- 6" x 14" (15 cm x 36 cm) piece of white solid fabric

BLOCK B
- 13" x 8" (33 cm x 20 cm) piece of blue print fabric
- 19" x 13" (48 cm x 33 cm) piece of tan print fabric
- 12" x 6" (30 cm x 15 cm) piece of white solid fabric

BLOCK C
- 9" x 10" (23 cm x 25 cm) piece of light blue print fabric
- 9" x 4" (23 cm x 10 cm) piece of blue-grey fabric
- 12" x 7" (30 cm x 18 cm) piece of white solid fabric
- Scrap of black solid fabric
- 12" x 4" (30 cm x 10 cm) piece of green print fabric
- Scrap of red print fabric

BLOCK D
- 14" x 14" (36 cm x 36 cm) piece of cream and red print fabric
- 6" x 2" (15 cm x 5 cm) piece of blue striped fabric
- 9" x 10" (23 cm x 25 cm) piece of blue checked fabric

You will also need:
- White, black, and orange embroidery floss
- White glass seed beads
- 3 – $^5/_{16}$" (8 mm) black sew-on snaps
- Paper-backed fusible web
- Stabilizer
- Lightwight copy paper or tying paper

CUTTING OUT THE PIECES
*Refer to **Preparing Fusible Appliqué Pieces**, page 101, and use patterns on pages 14 – 15 to cut out appliqué pieces. Background pieces are cut larger than needed and will be trimmed after appliqués and embroidery are added. All other measurements include a $^1/_4$" seam allowance.*

BLOCK A
From red print fabric:
- Cut 3 **strips** $1^1/_2$" x 12".

From white solid fabric:
- Cut 3 **strips** $1^1/_2$" x 12".

BLOCK B
From blue print fabric:
- Cut 2 **large squares** $3^1/_4$" x $3^1/_4$".
- Cut 4 **medium squares** $2^7/_8$" x $2^7/_8$".

From tan print fabric:
- Cut 1 **background square** $8^1/_2$" x $8^1/_2$".
- Cut 2 **large squares** $3^1/_4$" x $3^1/_4$".
- Cut 4 **medium squares** $2^7/_8$" x $2^7/_8$".
- Cut 4 **small squares** $2^1/_2$" x $2^1/_2$".

From white solid fabric:
- Cut 4 **small squares** $2^1/_2$" x $2^1/_2$".
- Cut 1 **snowflake** from pattern.

BLOCK C
From light blue print fabric:
- Cut 1 **background rectangle** $8^1/_2$" x $9^1/_2$".

From blue-grey print fabric:
- Cut 1 **ground** from pattern.

From white solid fabric:
- Cut 1 **strip** $1^1/_2$" x 11".
- Cut 1 **snowman** from pattern.

From black solid fabric:
- Cut 1 **hat** from pattern.

From green print fabric:
- Cut 1 **strip** $1^1/_2$" x 11".
- Cut 1 **rectangle** $1^1/_2$" x $6^1/_2$".

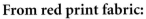

From red print fabric:
- Cut 1 **heart** from pattern.

BLOCK D
From cream and red print fabric:
- Cut 4 **rectangles** $1^1/2$" x $3^1/2$".
- Cut 6 **squares** $1^1/2$" x $1^1/2$".

From blue striped fabric:
- Cut 3 **squares** $1^1/2$" x $1^1/2$".

Reserve blue checked and remaining cream and red print fabrics for paper piecing.

MAKING SECTION 1

*Follow **Piecing**, page 99, **Pressing**, page 100, and **Appliqué**, page 101, to make **Section 1**.*

BLOCK A
Size (including seam allowance): $13^1/2$" x $3^1/2$"

1. Sew 2 red **strips** and 1 white **strip** together to make **Strip Set A**. Cut across **Strip Set A** at $1^1/2$" intervals to make 7 **Unit 1's**.

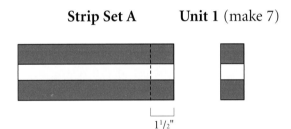

Strip Set A   **Unit 1** (make 7)

$1^1/2$"

2. Sew 2 white **strips** and 1 red **strip** together to make **Strip Set B**. Cut across **Strip Set B** at $1^1/2$" intervals to make 6 **Unit 2's**.

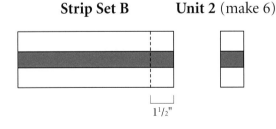

Strip Set B   **Unit 2** (make 6)

$1^1/2$"

3. Sew 7 **Unit 1's** and 6 **Unit 2's** together to make **Block A**.

Block A

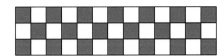

BLOCK B
Size (including seam allowance): $10^1/2$" x $10^1/2$"

1. Center and appliqué **snowflake** on **background square**. Randomly place and attach beads on **snowflake** using 1 strand of white floss.

2. Making sure **snowflake** is centered, trim background square to $6^1/2$" x $6^1/2$" to make **Unit 3**.

Unit 3

3. With right sides together, place 1 white **small square** on 1 corner of **Unit 3** and stitch diagonally (**Fig. 1**). Trim $1/4$" from stitching line (**Fig. 2**). Open up and press, pressing seam allowances to darker fabric (**Fig. 3**).

Fig. 1   **Fig. 2**   **Fig. 3**

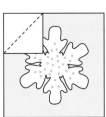
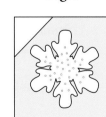

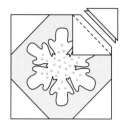

4. Continue adding white **small squares** to corners of **Unit 3** as shown in **Fig. 4**. Open up and press to complete **Unit 4**.

Fig. 4

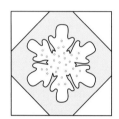

Unit 4

5. Draw diagonal line (corner to corner) on wrong side of each tan **medium square**. With right sides together, place 1 tan **medium square** on top of 1 blue **medium square**. Stitch seam ¼" from each side of drawn line (**Fig. 5**).

Fig. 5

6. Cut along drawn line and press open to make 2 **Small Triangle-Squares**. Repeat with remaining **medium squares** to make 8 **Small Triangle-Squares**.

Small Triangle-Squares (make 8)

7. Draw diagonal lines from corner to corner in both directions on wrong side of each tan **large square**. With right sides together, place 1 tan **large square** on top of 1 blue **large square**. Stitch seam ¼" from each side of 1 drawn line (**Fig. 6**).

Fig. 6

8. Cut along drawn line and press open to make 2 **Large Triangle-Squares**. Repeat with remaining **large squares** to make 4 **Large Triangle-Squares**.

Large Triangle-Squares (make 4)

9. On wrong side of 1 **Large Triangle-Square**, extend drawn line from corner of tan triangle to corner of blue triangle.

10. Match 2 **Large Triangle-Squares** with contrasting fabrics facing and marked unit on top. Stitch seam ¼" on each side of drawn line (**Fig. 7**). Cut apart along drawn line between stitching to make 2 **Hourglass Units**; press **Hourglass Units** open. Make 4 **Hourglass Units**.

Fig. 7

Hourglass Units (make 4)

10

11. Sew 2 **Small Triangle-Squares** and 1 **Hourglass Unit** together to make **Unit 5**. Make 4 **Unit 5's**.

Unit 5 (make 4)

12. Sew 2 tan **small squares** and 1 **Unit 5** together to make **Unit 6**. Make 2 **Unit 6's**.

Unit 6 (make 2)

13. Sew **Unit 4** and 2 **Unit 5's** together to make **Unit 7**.

Unit 7

14. Sew **Unit 7** and 2 **Unit 6's** together to make **Block B**.

Block B

BLOCK C

Size (including seam allowance): $6^1/_2$" x $10^1/_2$"

1. Matching side and bottom raw edges of **ground** appliqué piece and **background rectangle**, arrange appliqué pieces onto **background rectangle**; appliqué in place. Add machine Satin Stitched details for hat brim, arms, and feet.
2. Stem Stitch mouth using 2 strands of black floss, and add French Knot eyes using 6 strands of black floss. Satin Stitch carrot nose using 3 strands of orange floss. Add 3 black sew-on snaps for buttons.
3. Making sure **snowman** is centered, trim **background rectangle** to $6^1/_2$" x $7^1/_2$" to make **Unit 8**.

Unit 8

4. Sew 1 green **strip** and 1 white **strip** together to make **Strip Set C**. Cut across **Strip Set C** at $1^1/_2$" intervals to make 6 **Unit 9's**.

Strip Set C   **Unit 9** (make 6)

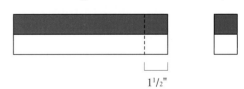

$1^1/_2$"

5. Sew 6 **Unit 9's** together to make **Unit 10**.

Unit 10

6. Sew **Unit 8**, **Unit 10**, and **rectangle** together to make **Block C**.

Block C

BLOCK D
Size (including seam allowance): 16$\frac{1}{2}$" x 3$\frac{1}{2}$"
1. Sew 2 cream and red print **squares** and 1 blue striped **square** together to make **Unit 11**. Make 3 **Unit 11's**.

Unit 11 (make 3)

2. For paper piecing foundations, use a fine-point marker and ruler to trace **Unit 12** pattern on page 15 onto paper. Make 6 traced patterns; cut out.
3. Rough cut a piece of blue checked fabric at least $\frac{1}{2}$" larger on all sides than area 1 on the traced pattern (foundation).
4. Place fabric piece right side down; place foundation right side up on top of fabric piece making sure fabric extends at least $\frac{1}{2}$" beyond all sides of area 1. Pin or glue fabric in place (**Fig. 8**).

Fig. 8

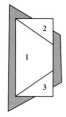

5. Rough cut a piece of cream and red fabric for area 2, making sure fabric will completely cover area. Turning foundation and fabric #1 over so that unmarked side of foundation is facing up, place fabric #2 on fabric #1, matching right sides. Pin fabric pieces in place (**Fig. 9**).

Fig. 9

6. Turn foundation and fabric pieces over so that marked side of foundation is facing up; sew along line between areas 1 and 2, sewing a few stitches beyond beginning and end of line (**Fig. 10**).

Fig. 10

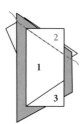

7. Fold foundation at seam and using ruler and rotary cutter, trim fabric pieces $\frac{1}{4}$" from seam (**Fig. 11**).

Fig. 11

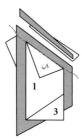

8. Unfold foundation, and turn foundation and fabric pieces over so that unmarked side of foundation is facing up. Open out piece #2; press (**Fig. 12**).

Fig. 12

9. Continue in the same manner to cover area 3 with a piece of cream and red fabric. Using ruler and rotary cutter, trim fabric ¼" from outer edge of foundation as indicated by red line in **Fig. 13**. Carefully tear away foundation paper to make **Unit 12**. Make 6 **Unit 12's**.

Fig. 13

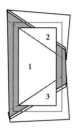

Unit 12 (make 6)

10. Sew 2 **Unit 12's** and 1 **Unit 11** together to make **Unit 13**. Make 3 **Unit 13's**.

Unit 13 (make 3)

11. Sew 3 **Unit 13's** and 4 **rectangles** together to make **Block D**.

Block D

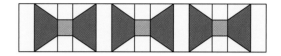

SECTION 1

1. Sew **Block B** and **Block C** together. Add **Block D**, then **Block A** to complete **Section 1**.

Section 1

13

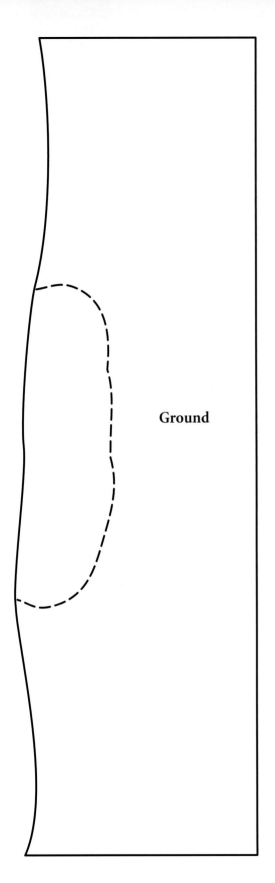

Ground

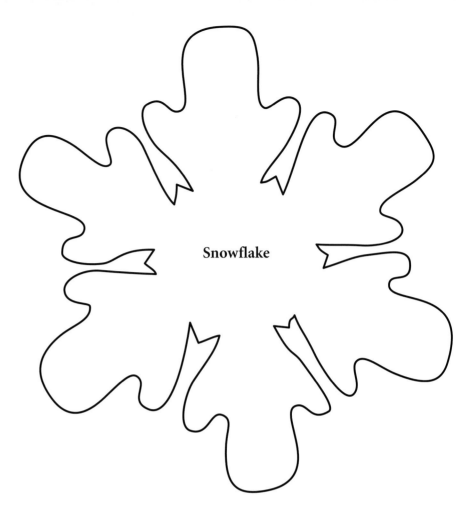

Snowflake

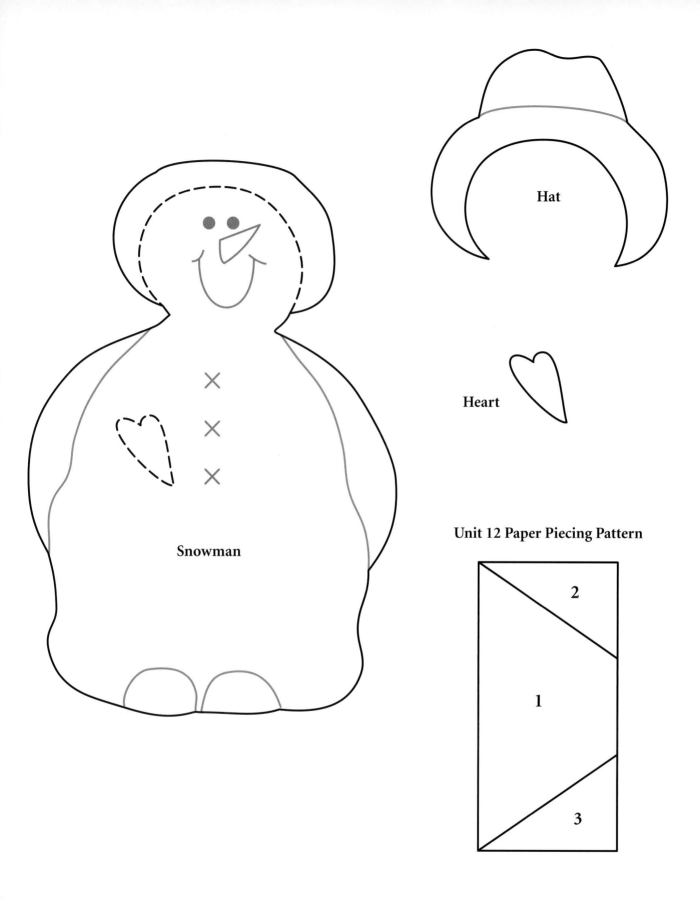

Hat

Heart

Snowman

Unit 12 Paper Piecing Pattern

2

1

3

SECTION 2

Size (including seam allowance): 16¹/2" x 13¹/2"

YARDAGE REQUIREMENTS
BLOCK A
8" x 6" (20 cm x 15 cm) piece of red plaid fabric

5" x 9" (13 cm x 23 cm) piece of green print fabric

10" x 6" (25 cm x 15 cm) piece of blue print fabric

9" x 9" (23 cm x 23 cm) piece of tan print fabric

BLOCK B
8" x 6" (20 cm x 15 cm) piece of cream and red print fabric

9" x 14" (23 cm x 36 cm) piece of multi-colored print fabric

8" x 6" (20 cm x 15 cm) piece of red print fabric

8" x 10" (20 cm x 25 cm) piece of cream and pink print fabric

Scrap of white solid fabric

BLOCK C
14" x 7" (36 cm x 18 cm) piece of tan and white striped fabric

Scrap each of 3 red print fabrics

You will also need:

Black embroidery floss

Paper-backed fusible web

Stabilizer

CUTTING OUT THE PIECES
*Refer to **Preparing Fusible Appliqué Pieces**, page 101, and use patterns on page 19 to cut out appliqué pieces. Background pieces are cut larger than needed and will be trimmed after appliqués and embroidery are added. All other measurements include a 1/4" seam allowance.*

BLOCK A
From red plaid fabric:
- Cut 2 **large squares** 3¹/2" x 3¹/2".
- Cut 1 **rectangle** 6¹/2" x 1¹/2".

From green print fabric:
- Cut 8 **small squares** 2" x 2".

From blue print fabric:
- Cut 2 squares 4¹/4" x 4¹/4". Cut squares *twice* diagonally to make 8 **small triangles**.

From tan print fabric:
- Cut 4 squares 3⁷/8" x 3⁷/8". Cut squares *once* diagonally to make 8 **large triangles**.

BLOCK B
From cream and red print fabric:
- Cut 4 **small rectangles** 1¹/2" x 4¹/2".

From multi-colored print fabric:
- Cut 1 **background square** 6¹/2" x 6¹/2".
- Cut 2 **large squares** 2⁷/8" x 2⁷/8".
- Cut 4 **small rectangles** 1¹/2" x 4¹/2".

From red print fabric:
- Cut 2 **large squares** 2⁷/8" x 2⁷/8".
- Cut 4 **small squares** 1¹/2" x 1¹/2".
- Cut 1 **small heart** from pattern.

From cream and pink print fabric:
- Cut 4 **large rectangles** 1¹/2" x 8¹/2".

From white solid fabric:
- Cut 1 **envelope** from pattern.

BLOCK C
From tan and white striped fabric:
- Cut 1 **background rectangle** $12^{1}/_{2}$" x $5^{1}/_{2}$".

From *each* red print fabric:
- Cut 1 **large heart** from pattern for a total of 3 **large hearts**.

MAKING SECTION 2
*Follow **Piecing**, page 99, **Pressing**, page 100, and **Appliqué**, page 101, to make **Section 2**.*

BLOCK A
Size (including seam allowance): $6^{1}/_{2}$" x $13^{1}/_{2}$"

1. With right sides together, place 1 **small square** on 1 corner of 1 **large square** and stitch diagonally (**Fig. 1**). Trim $^{1}/_{4}$" from stitching line (**Fig. 2**). Open up and press, pressing seam allowances to darker fabric (**Fig. 3**).

Fig. 1

Fig. 2

Fig. 3

2. Continuing adding **small squares** to corners of **large square** as shown in **Fig. 4**. Open up and press to complete **Unit 1**. Make 2 **Unit 1's**.

Fig. 4

Unit 1 (make 2)

3. Sew 1 **Unit 1** and 4 **small triangles** together to make **Unit 2**. Make 2 **Unit 2's**.

Unit 2 (make 2)

4. Sew 1 **Unit 2** and 4 **large triangles** together to make **Unit 3**. Make 2 **Unit 3's**.

Unit 3 (make 2)

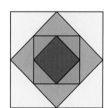

5. Sew 2 **Unit 3's** and **rectangle** together to make **Block A**.

Block A

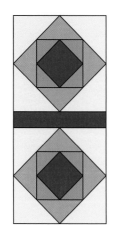

BLOCK B

Size (including seam allowance): 10¹/₂" x 10¹/₂"

1. Appliqué **envelope** and **small heart** on **background square**. Add machine Satin Stitched detail for envelope flap. Lightly trace or write *"My Valentine"* on envelope using sharp pencil. Stem Stitch words using 1 strand of black floss.

2. Making sure appliquéd design is centered, trim **background square** to 4¹/₂" x 4¹/₂" to make **Unit 4**.

Unit 4

3. Draw diagonal line (corner to corner) on wrong side of each multi-colored print **large square**. With right sides together, place 1 multi-colored print **large square** on top of 1 red print **large square**. Stitch seam ¹/₄" from each side of drawn line (**Fig. 5**).

Fig. 5

4. Cut along drawn line and press open to make 2 **Triangle-Squares**. Repeat with remaining **large squares** to make 4 **Triangle-Squares**.

Triangle-Squares (make 4)

5. Sew 1 cream and red print **small rectangle** and 1 multi-colored print **small rectangle** together to make **Unit 5**. Make 4 **Unit 5's**.

Unit 5 (make 4)

6. Sew 1 **Triangle-Square** to each end of 2 **Unit 5's** to make 2 **Unit 6's**.

Unit 6 (make 2)

7. Sew **Unit 4** and 2 **Unit 5's** together to make **Unit 7**.

Unit 7

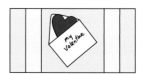

8. Sew **Unit 7** and 2 **Unit 6's** together to make **Unit 8**.

Unit 8

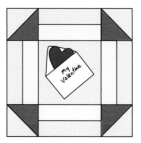

9. Sew 1 **small square** to each end of 2 **large rectangles** to make **Unit 9**. Make 2 **Unit 9's**.

Unit 9 (make 2)

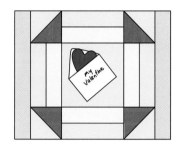

10. Sew **Unit 8** and 2 **large rectangles** together to make **Unit 10**.

Unit 10

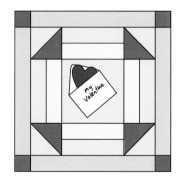

11. Sew **Unit 10** and 2 **Unit 9's** together to make **Block B**.

Block B

BLOCK C
Size (including seam allowance): 10^1/$_2$" x 3^1/$_2$"
1. Spacing hearts ^{1}/$_4$" apart, appliqué **large hearts** on **background rectangle**.
2. Making sure appliquéd **large hearts** are centered, trim **background rectangle** to 10^1/$_2$" x 3^1/$_2$" to make **Block C**.

Block C

SECTION 2
1. Sew **Block B** and **Block C** together. Add **Block A** to complete **Section 2**.

Section 2

Large Heart

Small Heart

Envelope

SECTION 3

Size (including seam allowance): $9^1/_2$" x $13^1/_2$"

YARDAGE REQUIREMENTS

12" x 11" (30 cm x 28 cm) piece of light blue print fabric

11" x 9" (28 cm x 23 cm) piece of medium green print fabric

11" x 9" (28 cm x 23 cm) piece of white solid fabric

6" x 4" (15 cm x 10 cm) piece of cream solid fabric

6" x 4" (15 cm x 10 cm) piece of orange print fabric

Scraps of yellow, dark green, and red print fabrics

You will also need:

White embroidery floss

Paper-backed fusible web

Stabilizer

CUTTING OUT THE PIECES

*Refer to **Preparing Fusible Appliqué Pieces**, page 101, and use patterns on page 22 to cut out appliqué pieces. The background rectangle is cut larger than needed and will be trimmed after appliqués and embroidery are added. All other measurements include a $^1/_4$" seam allowance.*

From light blue print fabric:
- Cut 1 **background rectangle** $8^1/_2$" x $9^1/_2$".
- Cut 1 **large rectangle** $9^1/_2$" x $1^1/_2$".

From medium green print fabric:
- Cut 12 **squares** $2^3/_8$" x $2^3/_8$".

From white solid fabric:
- Cut 12 **squares** $2^3/_8$" x $2^3/_8$".

From cream solid fabric:
- Cut 3 **small rectangles** $2^1/_2$" x $1^1/_2$".

From orange print fabric:
- Cut 3 **small rectangles** $2^1/_2$" x $1^1/_2$".

From yellow print fabric:
- Cut 1 **kite** from pattern.

From dark green print fabric:
- Cut 1 **shamrock** from pattern.

From red print fabric:
- Cut 3 **ties** (for kite tail) from pattern.

MAKING SECTION 3

*Follow **Piecing**, page 99, **Pressing**, page 100, and **Appliqué**, page 101, to make **Section 3**.*

1. Arrange **kite**, **shamrock**, and **ties** on **background rectangle**. *(**Note:** Make sure appliqué design fits into a 6" x 7" area.)* Appliqué pieces in place. Lightly mark kite tail with sharp pencil making sure tail goes through center of each tie. Stem Stitch kite tail using 3 strands of white floss.

2. Making sure appliquéd design is centered, trim **background rectangle** to 6½" x 7½" to make **Unit 1**.

Unit 1

3. Draw diagonal line (corner to corner) on wrong side of each white **square**. With right sides together, place 1 white **square** on top of 1 medium green **square**. Stitch seam ¼" from each side of drawn line (**Fig. 1**).

Fig. 1

4. Cut along drawn line and press open to make 2 **Triangle-Squares**. Repeat with remaining **squares** to make 24 **Triangle-Squares**.

Triangle-Squares (make 24)

5. Sew 4 **Triangle-Squares** together to make **Unit 2**. Make 6 **Unit 2's**.

Unit 2 (make 6)

6. Sew 3 **Unit 2's** together to make **Unit 3**. Make 2 **Unit 3's**.

Unit 3 (make 2)

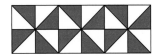

7. Sew 1 cream **small rectangle** and 1 orange **small rectangle** together to make **Unit 4**. Make 3 **Unit 4's**.

Unit 4 (make 3)

8. Sew 3 **Unit 4's** together to make **Unit 5**.

Unit 5

9. Sew **Unit 1** and **Unit 5** together to make **Unit 6**.

Unit 6

10. Sew 1 **Unit 3** and **Unit 6** together to make **Unit 7**.

Unit 7

11. Sew 1 **Unit 3**, **Unit 7**, and **large rectangle** together to complete **Section 3**.

Section 3

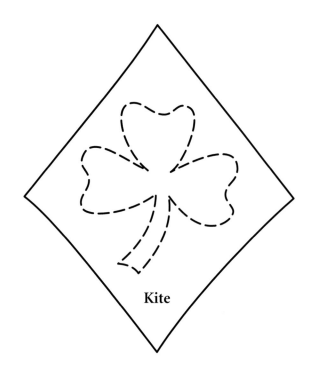

Kite

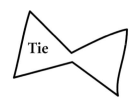

Tie

Shamrock

SECTION 4

Size (including seam allowance): $9^1/2$" x $13^1/2$"

YARDAGE REQUIREMENTS
BLOCK A
- 10" x 6" (25 cm x 15 cm) piece of coral print fabric
- 10" x 6" (25 cm x 15 cm) piece of white solid fabric

BLOCK B
- 7" x 5" (18 cm x 13 cm) piece of light blue print fabric
- 7" x 5" (18 cm x 13 cm) piece of medium red print fabric
- 8" x 5" (20 cm x 13 cm) piece of dark red print fabric
- 7" x 8" (18 cm x 20 cm) piece of medium gold print fabric
- 6" x 8" (15 cm x 20 cm) piece of dark blue print fabric
- 10" x 2" (25 cm x 5 cm) piece of dark green print fabric
- 6" x 5" (15 cm x 13 cm) piece of white solid fabric
- Scraps of dark gold plaid, dark gold print, black solid, red polka dot, and medium green print fabrics

You will also need:
- Paper-backed fusible web
- Stabilizer

CUTTING OUT THE PIECES
*Refer to **Preparing Fusible Appliqué Pieces**, page 101, and use patterns on page 25 to cut out appliqué pieces. Follow **Template Cutting**, page 99, to make templates from patterns A – C on page 26. All measurements include a $1/4$" seam allowance.*

BLOCK A
From coral print fabric:
- Cut 3 **strips** $1^1/2$" x 9".

From white solid fabric:
- Cut 3 **strips** $1^1/2$" x 9".

BLOCK B
From light blue print fabric:
- Cut 1 **A** and 1 **A reversed** from template.

From medium red print fabric:
- Cut 1 **B** from template.

From dark red print fabric:
- Cut 1 **C** from template.

From medium gold print fabric:
- Cut 1 **large rectangle** $5^1/2$" x $6^1/2$".

From dark blue print fabric:
- Cut 1 **small rectangle** $4^1/2$" x $6^1/2$".

From dark green print fabric:
- Cut 1 **long rectangle** $9^1/2$" x $1^1/2$".

From white solid fabric:
- Cut 1 **large flower center** from pattern.
- Cut 2 **small flower centers** from pattern.
- Cut 1 **roof trim** from pattern.

From dark gold plaid fabric:
- Cut 1 **upper door** $1^1/2$" x $1^1/2$" for appliqué.

From dark gold print fabric:
- Cut 1 **lower door** $1^1/2$" x 3" for appliqué.

From black solid fabric:
- Cut 2 **windows** $1^1/4$" x 2" for appliqué.

From red polka dot fabric:
- Cut 1 **large flower** from pattern.
- Cut 2 **small flowers** from pattern.

From medium green print fabric:
- Cut 6 **leaves** from pattern.
- Cut 1 **small bush** from pattern.
- Cut 1 **large bush** from pattern.

MAKING SECTION 4

*Follow **Piecing**, page 99, **Pressing**, page 100, and **Appliqué**, page 101, to make **Section 4.***

BLOCK A

Size (including seam allowance): $9^1/_2$" x $3^1/_2$"

1. Sew 2 white **strips** and 1 coral **strip** together to make **Strip Set A**. Cut across **Strip Set A** at $1^1/_2$" intervals to make 5 **Unit 1's**.

Strip Set A   **Unit 1** (make 5)

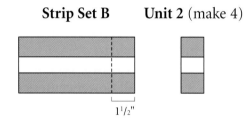

$1^1/_2$"

2. Sew 2 coral **strips** and 1 white **strip** together to make **Strip Set B**. Cut across **Strip Set B** at $1^1/_2$" intervals to make 4 **Unit 2's**.

Strip Set B   **Unit 2** (make 4)

$1^1/_2$"

3. Sew 5 **Unit 1's** and 4 **Unit 2's** together to make **Block A**.

Block A

BLOCK B

Size (including seam allowance): $9^1/_2$" x $10^1/_2$"

1. Matching dots, sew **A** and **B** together. Sew **C** to **B**, then **A reversed** to **C** to make **Unit 3**.

Unit 3

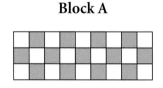

2. Sew **large rectangle** and **small rectangle** together to make **Unit 4**.

Unit 4

3. Sew **Unit 3** and **Unit 4** together to make **Unit 5**.

Unit 5

4. Matching raw edges of **lower door** and **bushes** with bottom edge of **Unit 5**, arrange appliqué pieces on **Unit 5**. Upper door should overlap lower door $^1/_4$". *(Be sure to allow for seam allowance on left side and top of **Unit 5**. Seam allowance is indicated by dashed line in diagram.)* Appliqué pieces in place to make **Unit 6**.

Unit 6

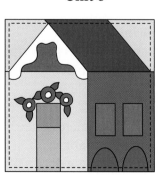

5. Sew **Unit 6** and **long rectangle** together to make **Block B**.

Large Flower

Large Flower Center

Block B

Large Bush

Section 4

1. Sew **Block A** and **Block B** together to complete **Section 4**.

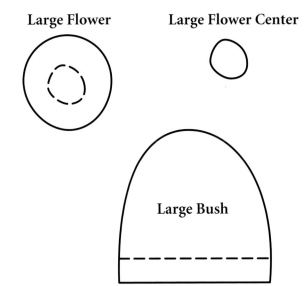

Small Bush

Section 4

Small Flower

Roof Trim

Leaf

Small Flower Center

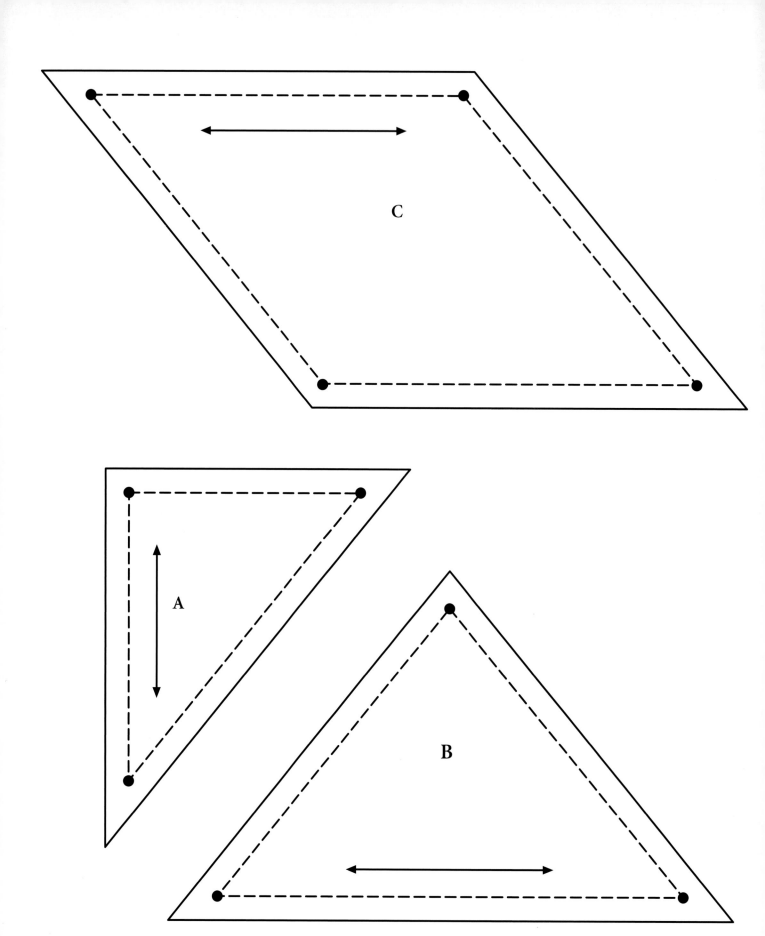

SECTION 5

Size (including seam allowance): 17¹/₂" x 13¹/₂"

Size (including seam allowance): $17^1/_2$" x $13^1/_2$"

YARDAGE REQUIREMENTS

BLOCK A

14" x 10" (36 cm x 25 cm) piece of light blue print fabric

14" x 5" (36 cm x 13 cm) piece of light green print fabric

Scraps of purple, pink, dark green, yellow, and medium blue print fabrics

BLOCK B's

13" x 12" (33 cm x 30 cm) piece of yellow print fabric

4" x 7" (10 cm x 18 cm) piece of light blue print fabric

4" x 10" (10 cm x 25 cm) piece of pink print fabric

4" x 7" (10 cm x 18 cm) piece of medium blue print fabric

7" x 8" (18 cm x 20 cm) piece of green print fabric

BLOCK C

6" x 8" (15 cm x 20 cm) piece of red print fabric

6" x 8" (15 cm x 20 cm) piece of white solid fabric

BLOCK D

9" x 6" (23 cm x 15 cm) piece of cream print fabric

7" x 4" (18 cm x 10 cm) piece of light blue print fabric

2" x 7" (5 cm x 18 cm) piece of green print fabric

Scraps of cream and blue print and medium blue print fabrics

You will also need:

Paper-backed fusible web

Stabilizer

CUTTING OUT THE PIECES

*Refer to **Preparing Fusible Appliqué Pieces**, page 101, and use patterns on pages 32 – 33 to cut appliqué pieces. The background rectangle of **Block A** is cut larger than needed and will be trimmed after appliqués are added. All other measurements include a $^1/_4$" seam allowance.*

BLOCK A

From light blue print fabric:

- Cut 1 **background rectangle** $12^1/_2$" x $8^1/_2$".

From light green print fabric:

- Cut 1 **ground** from pattern.

From purple print fabric:

- Cut 1 **fence post #1** and 1 **fence post #1 reversed** from pattern.
- Cut 1 **fence post #2** and 1 **fence post #2 reversed** from pattern.
- Cut 1 **fence rail** and 1 **fence rail reversed** from pattern.

From pink print fabric:

- Cut 1 **rabbit** from pattern.

From dark green print fabric:

- Cut 4 **leaves** from pattern.

From yellow print fabric:

- Cut 2 **flowers** from pattern.

From medium blue print fabric:

- Cut 2 **flower centers** from pattern.

BLOCK B's

From yellow print fabric:

- Cut 1 **large square** $2^7/_8$" x $2^7/_8$".
- Cut 2 **medium squares** $2^1/_2$" x $2^1/_2$".
- Cut 8 **small squares** $1^1/_2$" x $1^1/_2$".
- Cut 4 **large rectangles** $4^1/_2$" x $2^1/_2$".

From light blue print fabric:

- Cut 2 **small rectangles** $1^1/_2$" x $3^1/_2$".
- Cut 2 **smallest rectangles** $1^1/_2$" x $2^1/_2$".

From pink print fabric:

- Cut 2 **medium rectangles** $1^1/_2$" x $4^1/_2$".
- Cut 2 **small rectangles** $1^1/_2$" x $3^1/_2$".

From medium blue print fabric:
- Cut 1 **large square** $2^7/8$" x $2^7/8$".
- Cut 2 **small squares** $1^1/2$" x $1^1/2$".

From green print fabric:
- Cut 4 **long rectangles** $1^1/2$" x $6^1/2$".

BLOCK C
From red print fabric:
- Cut 3 **strips** $1^1/2$" x 7".

From white solid fabric:
- Cut 3 **strips** $1^1/2$" x 7".

BLOCK D
From cream print fabric:
- Cut 2 **squares** $2^1/2$" x $2^1/2$".
- Cut 1 square $4^7/8$" x $4^7/8$". Cut square *once* diagonally to make 2 **large triangles**.

From light blue print fabric:
- Cut 2 squares $2^7/8$" x $2^7/8$". Cut square *once* diagonally to make 4 **small triangles**.

From green print fabric:
- Cut 1 **rectangle** $1^1/2$" x $6^1/2$".

From cream and blue print fabric:
- Cut 1 **square** $2^1/2$" x $2^1/2$".

From medium blue print fabric:
- Cut 1 **basket handle** from pattern.

MAKING SECTION 5
*Follow **Piecing**, page 99, **Pressing**, page 100, and **Appliqué**, page 101, to make **Section 5**.*

BLOCK A
Size (including seam allowance): $10^1/2$" x $6^1/2$"
1. Matching side and bottom raw edges of **ground** and **background rectangle**, appliqué **ground**, **rabbit**, **fence pieces**, **leaves**, **flowers**, and **flower centers** to **background rectangle**.
2. Referring to photo, page 27, and **Block A** diagram for placement, trim **background rectangle** to $10^1/2$" x $6^1/2$" to make **Block A**.

Block A

BLOCK B's
Size (including seam allowance): $7^1/2$" x $7^1/2$"
*Note: You will make 2 **Block B's** which are mirror images of each other.*
1. With right sides together, place 1 yellow **small square** on 1 end of 1 light blue **smallest rectangle** and stitch diagonally. Trim $1/4$" from stitching line. Open up and press, pressing seam allowances to darker fabric to make **Unit 1a**. Make **Unit 1b** in the same manner, but with stitching made in different direction as shown.

Unit 1a

Unit 1b

2. Repeat Step 1 to make **Unit 2a** and **Unit 2b** using yellow **small squares** and light blue **small rectangles**.

Unit 2a	Unit 2b

3. Repeat Step 1 to make **Unit 3a** and **Unit 3b** using yellow **small squares** and pink **small rectangles**.

Unit 3a	Unit 3b

4. Repeat Step 1 to make **Unit 4a** and **Unit 4b** using yellow **small squares** and pink **medium rectangles**.

Unit 4a	Unit 4b

5. Sew **Unit 1a** and 1 **medium square** together to make **Unit 5a**. Sew **Unit 1b** and 1 **medium square** together to make **Unit 5b**.

Unit 5a   **Unit 5b**

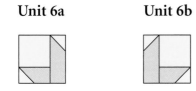

6. Sew **Unit 5a** and **Unit 2a** together to make **Unit 6a**. Sew **Unit 5b** and **Unit 2b** together to make **Unit 6b**.

Unit 6a   **Unit 6b**

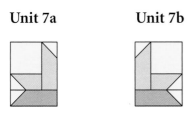

7. Sew **Unit 6a** and **Unit 3a** together to make **Unit 7a**. Sew **Unit 6b** and **Unit 3b** together to make **Unit 7b**.

Unit 7a   **Unit 7b**

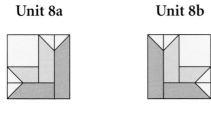

8. Sew **Unit 7a** and **Unit 4a** together to make **Unit 8a**. Sew **Unit 7b** and **Unit 4b** together to make **Unit 8b**.

Unit 8a   **Unit 8b**

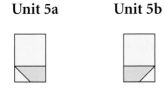

9. Sew **Unit 8a** and 1 **large rectangle** together to make **Unit 9a**. Sew **Unit 8b** and 1 **large rectangle** together to make **Unit 9b**.

Unit 9a   **Unit 9b**

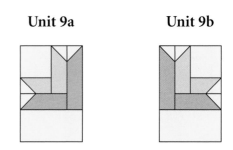

10. Draw diagonal line (corner to corner) on wrong side of yellow **large square**. With right sides together, place yellow **large square** on top of medium blue **large square**. Stitch seam $1/4$" from each side of drawn line (**Fig. 1**).

Fig. 1

11. Cut along drawn line and press open to make 2 **Triangle-Squares**.

Triangle-Squares (make 2)

12. Sew 1 **Triangle-Square** and 1 **large rectangle** together to make **Unit 10a**. Sew 1 **Triangle-Square** and 1 **large rectangle** together to make **Unit 10b**.

Unit 10a   **Unit 10b**

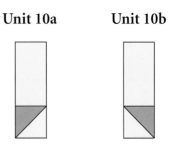

13. Sew **Unit 9a** and **Unit 10a** together to make **Unit 11a**. Sew **Unit 9b** and **Unit 10b** together to make **Unit 11b**.

Unit 11a   **Unit 11b**

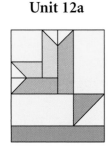   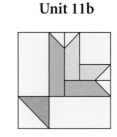

14. Sew **Unit 11a** and 1 **long rectangle** together to make **Unit 12a**. Sew **Unit 11b** and 1 **long rectangle** together to make **Unit 12b**.

Unit 12a   **Unit 12b**

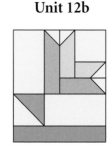

15. Sew 1 **long rectangle** and 1 medium blue **small square** together to make **Unit 13**. Make 2 **Unit 13's**.

Unit 13 (make 2)

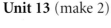

16. Sew **Unit 12a** and 1 **Unit 13** together to make **Block B-a**. Sew **Unit 12b** and 1 **Unit 13** together to make **Block B-b**.

Block B-a   **Block B-b**

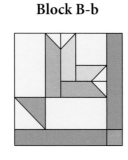

BLOCK C
Size (including seam allowance): $3^{1}/_{2}$" x $7^{1}/_{2}$"

1. Sew 2 red **strips** and 1 white **strip** together to make **Strip Set A**. Cut across **Strip Set A** at $1^{1}/_{2}$" intervals to make 4 **Unit 14's**.

Strip Set A   **Unit 14** (make 4)

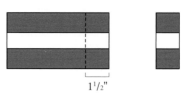

$1^{1}/_{2}$"

2. Sew 2 white **strips** and 1 red **strip** together to make **Strip Set B**. Cut across **Strip Set B** at $1^{1}/_{2}$" intervals to make 3 **Unit 15's**.

Strip Set B   **Unit 15** (make 3)

$1^{1}/_{2}$"

3. Sew 4 **Unit 14's** and 3 **Unit 15's** together to make **Block C**.

Block C

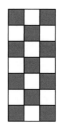

BLOCK D
Size (including seam allowance): $7^{1}/_{2}$" x $6^{1}/_{2}$"
1. Matching raw edges of bottom of handle and long side of triangle, appliqué **basket handle** to 1 **large triangle** to make **Unit 16**.

Unit 16

2. Sew 1 **small triangle** and 1 cream **square** together to make **Unit 17a**. Sew 1 **small triangle** and 1 cream **square** together to make **Unit 17b**.

Unit 17a   **Unit 17b**

3. Sew 2 **small triangles** and 1 cream and blue **square** together to make **Unit 18**.

Unit 18

4. Sew **Unit 18** and 1 **large triangle** together to make **Unit 19**.

Unit 19

5. Sew **Unit 19**, **Unit 17a**, and **Unit 17b** together to make **Unit 20**.

Unit 20

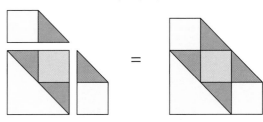

6. Sew **Unit 20** and **Unit 16** together to make **Unit 21**.

Unit 21

7. Sew **Unit 21** and 1 **rectangle** together to make **Block D**.

Block D

Section 5
1. Sew **Block B-a** and **Block C** together make **Unit 22**.

Unit 22

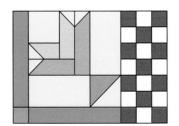

31

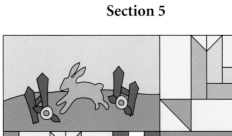

2. Sew **Block B-b** and **Block D** together make **Unit 23**.

3. Sew **Block A** and **Unit 22** together. Add **Unit 23** to complete **Section 5**.

Unit 23

Section 5

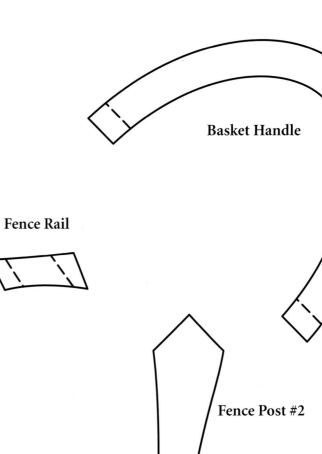

Flower

Leaf

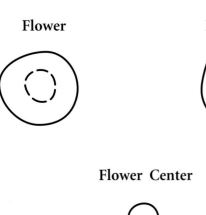

Flower Center

Fence Rail

Basket Handle

Fence Post #1

Fence Post #2

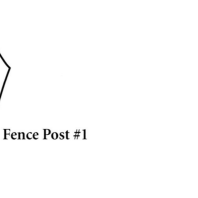

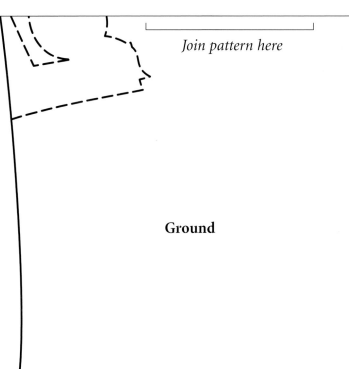

Ground

Join pattern here

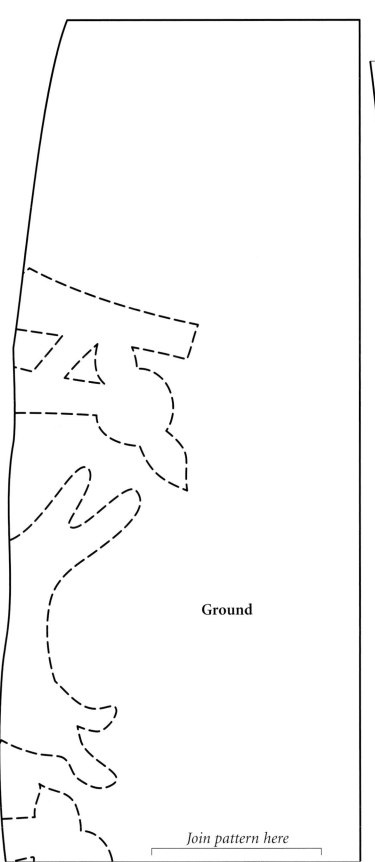

Ground

Join pattern here

Rabbit

SECTION 6

Size (including seam allowance): 9¹/₂" x 13¹/₂"

YARDAGE REQUIREMENTS
BLOCK A
11" x 14" (28 cm x 36 cm) piece of tan print fabric

5" x 8" (13 cm x 20 cm) piece of blue print fabric

Scraps of cream print, pink solid, medium brown print, and dark brown print fabrics

BLOCK B
11" x 7" (28 cm x 18 cm) piece of cream solid fabric

Scraps of orange print, green polka dot, yellow print, navy polka dot, dark green print, red print, and medium green print fabrics

BLOCK C
13" x 4" (33 cm x 10 cm) piece of red print fabric

13" x 4" (33 cm x 10 cm) piece of white solid fabric

You will also need:

White, black, pink, light green, medium green, and dark green embroidery floss

9 – ³/₈" (9.5 mm) diameter buttons of assorted colors

9" (23 cm) of ¹/₈" (3 mm) wide white satin ribbon

Paper-backed fusible web

Stabilizer

CUTTING OUT THE PIECES
*Refer to **Preparing Fusible Appliqué Pieces**, page 101, and use patterns on pages 36 – 37 to cut appliqué pieces. The background rectangles are cut larger than needed and will be trimmed after appliqués and embroidery are added. All other measurements include a ¹/₄" seam allowance.*

BLOCK A
From tan print fabric:
- Cut 1 **background rectangle** 9¹/₂" x 12¹/₂".

From blue print fabric:
- Cut 1 **dress** from pattern.

From cream print fabric:
- Cut 1 **wing** and 1 **wing reversed** from pattern.

From pink solid fabric:
- Cut 1 **face** from pattern.
- Cut 1 **foot** and 1 **foot reversed** from pattern.
- Cut 1 **hand** and 1 **hand reversed** from pattern.

From medium brown print fabric:
- Cut 1 **hair** from pattern.

From dark brown print fabric:
- Cut 1 **basket** from pattern.

BLOCK B
From cream solid fabric:
- Cut 1 **background rectangle** $9^{1}/_{2}$" x $5^{1}/_{2}$".

From orange print fabric:
- Cut 1 **carrot** from pattern.

From green polka dot fabric:
- Cut 1 **carrot leaves** from pattern.

From yellow print fabric:
- Cut 1 **flower** from pattern.

From navy polka dot fabric:
- Cut 1 **flower center** from pattern.

From dark green print fabric:
- Cut 1 **flower leaves** from pattern.

From red print fabric:
- Cut 1 **apple** from pattern.

From medium green print fabric:
- Cut 2 **apple leaves** from pattern.

BLOCK C
From red print fabric:
- Cut 2 **strips** $1^{1}/_{2}$" x 12".

From white solid fabric:
- Cut 2 **strips** $1^{1}/_{2}$" x 12".

MAKING SECTION 6

*Follow **Piecing**, page 99, **Pressing**, page 100, and **Appliqué**, page 101, to make **Section 6**.*

BLOCK A
Size (including seam allowance): $7^{1}/_{2}$" x $10^{1}/_{2}$"

1. Arrange **wings**, **feet**, **dress**, **face**, **hair**, **basket**, and **hands** on **background rectangle**; appliqué. Machine Satin Stitch arm details.
2. Make French Knot eyes using 3 strands of black floss. Add a Straight Stitch "highlight" using 1 strand of white floss in center of each French Knot. Make nose, mouth, and eyebrows using 1 strand of black floss and Straight Stitches. Add cheeks using 1 strand of pink floss and Straight Stitches. In random fashion, make Lazy Daisies for leaves in basket using 2 strands of light green for half and 2 strands of medium green for remainder; sew buttons on for flowers. Tack ribbon to angel and tie bow; knot and trim ends.

3. Making sure appliquéd design is centered, trim **background rectangle** to $7^{1}/_{2}$" x $10^{1}/_{2}$" to make **Block A**.

Block A

BLOCK B
Size (including seam allowance): $7^{1}/_{2}$" x $3^{1}/_{2}$"

1. Arrange **carrot**, **carrot leaves**, **flower**, **flower center**, **flower leaves**, **apple**, and **apple leaves** on **background rectangle**. *(**Note:** Make sure entire appliqué design is no wider than $6^{1}/_{2}$".)* Appliqué pieces in place. Lightly mark flower stem with sharp pencil making sure stem goes through center of leaves. Stem Stitch stem using 3 strands of dark green floss.
2. Making sure appliquéd design is centered, trim **background rectangle** to $7^{1}/_{2}$" x $3^{1}/_{2}$" to make **Block B**.

Block B

BLOCK C

Size (including seam allowance): $2^1/2$" x $13^1/2$"

1. Sew 1 white **strip** and 1 red **strip** together to make **Strip Set**. Make 2 **Strip Sets**. Cut across **Strip Sets** at $1^1/2$" intervals to make 13 **Unit 1's**.

Strip Set (make 2)   **Unit 1** (make 13)

$1^1/2$"

Face

2. Sew 13 **Unit 1's** together to make **Block C**.

Block C

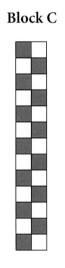

Dress

Section 6

1. Sew **Block A** and **Block B** together. Add **Block C** to complete **Section 6**.

Section 6

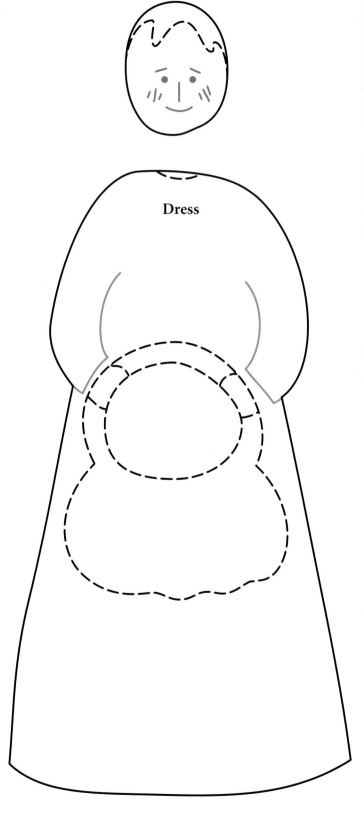

36

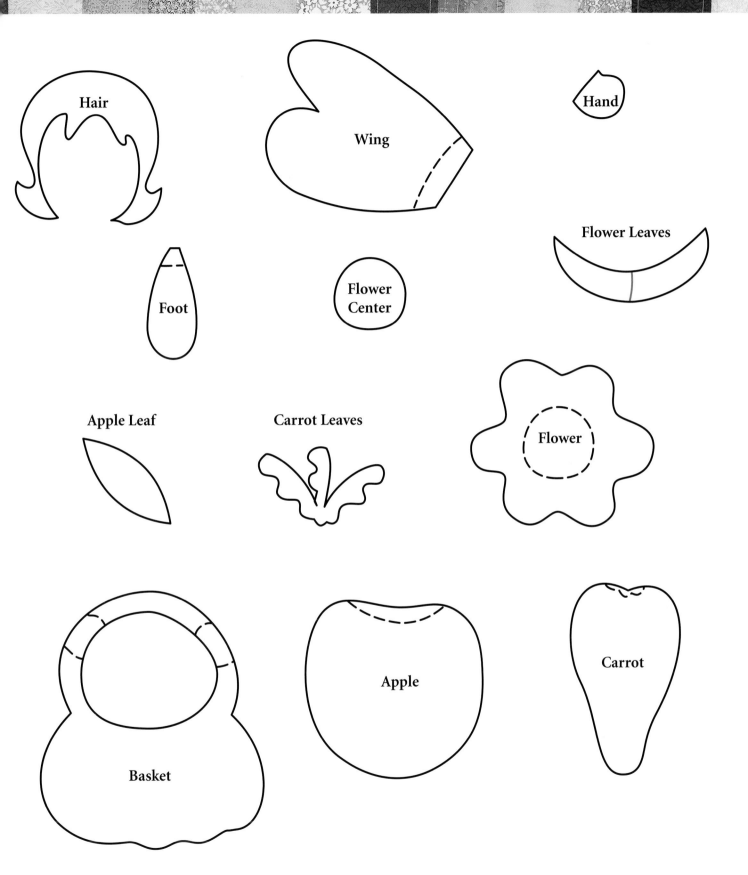

Hair

Wing

Hand

Flower Leaves

Foot

Flower Center

Apple Leaf

Carrot Leaves

Flower

Basket

Apple

Carrot

SECTION 7

Size (including seam allowance): 9$\frac{1}{2}$" x 13$\frac{1}{2}$"

YARDAGE REQUIREMENTS
BLOCK A
7" x 5" (18 cm x 13 cm) piece of royal blue print fabric

13" x 5" (33 cm x 13 cm) piece of white solid fabric

BLOCK B
10" x 10" (25 cm x 25 cm) piece of white solid fabric

6" x 4" (15 cm x 10 cm) piece of yellow print fabric

Scraps of gold print and pink polka dot fabrics

BLOCK C
13" x 10" (33 cm x 25 cm) piece of light green print fabric

8" x 3" (20 cm x 8 cm) piece of dark yellow print fabric

10" x 2" (25 cm x 5 cm) piece of royal blue print fabric

10" x 2" (25 cm x 5 cm) piece of white solid fabric

Scraps of light blue print, dark pink polka dot, yellow polka dot, and medium green print fabrics

You will also need:

Green embroidery floss

Paper-backed fusible web

Stabilizer

CUTTING OUT THE PIECES
*Refer to **Preparing Fusible Appliqué Pieces**, page 101, and use patterns on page 41 to cut appliqué pieces. The background pieces are cut larger than needed and will be trimmed after appliqués and embroidery are added. All other measurements include a $\frac{1}{4}$" seam allowance.*

BLOCK A
From royal blue print fabric:
- Cut 6 **large squares** 1$\frac{7}{8}$" x 1$\frac{7}{8}$".

From white solid fabric:
- Cut 6 **large squares** 1$\frac{7}{8}$" x 1$\frac{7}{8}$".
- Cut 6 **small squares** 1$\frac{1}{2}$" x 1$\frac{1}{2}$".

BLOCK B
From white solid fabric:
- Cut 1 **background square** 8$\frac{1}{2}$" x 8$\frac{1}{2}$".

From yellow print fabric:
- Cut 1 **bell** and 1 **bell reversed** from pattern.

From gold print fabric:
- Cut 2 **clappers** from pattern.

From pink polka dot fabric:
- Cut 1 **bow** from pattern.

38

BLOCK C
From light green print fabric:
- Cut 1 **background rectangle** 11$\frac{1}{2}$" x 8$\frac{1}{2}$".

From dark yellow print fabric:
- Cut 1 **ribbon** from pattern.

From royal blue print fabric:
- Cut 1 **strip** 1$\frac{1}{2}$" x 9".

From white solid fabric:
- Cut 1 **strip** 1$\frac{1}{2}$" x 9".

From light blue print fabric:
- Cut 2 **small flowers** from pattern.

From dark pink polka dot print fabric:
- Cut 1 **large flower** from pattern.

From yellow polka dot fabric:
- Cut 1 **large flower center** from pattern.
- Cut 2 **small flower centers** from pattern.

From medium green print fabric:
- Cut 1 **large leaf** and 1 **large leaf reversed** from pattern.
- Cut 1 **small leaf** and 1 **small leaf reversed** from pattern.

MAKING SECTION 7
*Follow **Piecing**, page 99, **Pressing**, page 100, and **Appliqué**, page 101, to make **Section 7**.*

BLOCK A
Size (including seam allowance): 3$\frac{1}{2}$" x 6$\frac{1}{2}$"

1. Draw diagonal line (corner to corner) on wrong side of each white **large square**. With right sides together, place 1 white **large square** on top of 1 royal blue **large square**. Stitch seam $\frac{1}{4}$" from each side of drawn line (**Fig. 1**).

Fig. 1

2. Cut along drawn line and press open to make 2 **Triangle-Squares**. Make 12 **Triangle-Squares**.

Triangle-Squares (make 12)

3. Sew 2 **Triangle-Squares** and 1 **small square** together to make **Unit 1**. Make 6 **Unit 1's**.

Unit 1 (make 6)

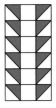

4. Sew 6 **Unit 1's** together to make **Block A**.

Block A

BLOCK B
Size (including seam allowance): 6$\frac{1}{2}$" x 6$\frac{1}{2}$"

1. Arrange **clappers**, **bells**, and **bow** on **background square**; appliqué. Machine Satin Stitch bow details.
2. Making sure appliquéd design is centered, trim **background square** to 6$\frac{1}{2}$" x 6$\frac{1}{2}$" to make **Block B**.

Block B

BLOCK C

Size (including seam allowance): $9^{1}/_{2}$" x $7^{1}/_{2}$"

1. Arrange **leaves, flowers, flower centers,** and **ribbon** on **background rectangle.** (***Note:*** *Make sure appliqué design fits into an $8^{1}/_{2}$" x $5^{1}/_{2}$" area.*) Appliqué pieces in place. Lightly mark flower stems with sharp pencil making sure stem goes through center of **ribbon.** Stem Stitch stems using 3 strands of green floss.

2. Making sure appliquéd and embroidered design is centered, trim **background rectangle** to $9^{1}/_{2}$" x $6^{1}/_{2}$" to make **Unit 2.**

Unit 2

3. Sew 1 royal blue **strip** and 1 white **strip** together to make **Strip Set.** Cut across **Strip Set** at $1^{1}/_{2}$" intervals to make 5 **Unit 3's.**

Strip Set   **Unit 3** (make 5)

$1^{1}/_{2}$"

4. Sew 5 **Unit 3's** together; remove 1 white square from end to make **Unit 4.**

Unit 4

5. Sew **Unit 2** and **Unit 4** together to make **Block C.**

Block C

Section 7

1. Sew **Block A** and **Block B** together. Add **Block C** to complete **Section 7.**

Section 7

40

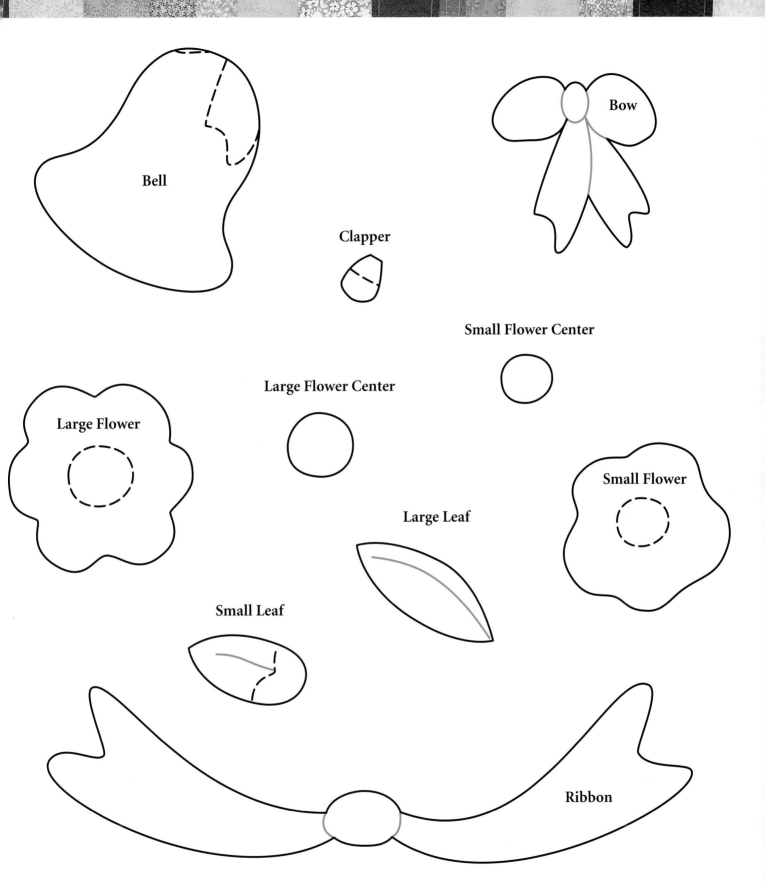

Bell

Bow

Clapper

Small Flower Center

Large Flower Center

Large Flower

Small Flower

Large Leaf

Small Leaf

Ribbon

SECTION 8

Size (including seam allowance): 8^1/$_2$" x 15^1/$_2$"

YARDAGE REQUIREMENTS
BLOCK A
12" x 12" (30 cm x 30 cm) piece of cream print fabric
8" x 6" (20 cm x 15 cm) piece of white solid fabric
8" x 8" (20 cm x 20 cm) piece of red polka dot fabric
Scraps of blue print, brown print, and green print fabrics

BLOCK B
12" x 12" (30 cm x 30 cm) piece of white solid fabric
12" x 6" (30 cm x 15 cm) piece of red print fabric
7" x 7" (18 cm x 18 cm) piece of blue and red striped fabric
7" x 7" (18 cm x 18 cm) piece of red and white striped fabric

You will also need:
Paper-backed fusible web
Stabilizer

CUTTING OUT THE PIECES
*Refer to **Preparing Fusible Appliqué Pieces**, page 101, and use patterns on page 45 to cut appliqué pieces. The background pieces are cut larger than needed and will be trimmed after appliqués are added. All other measurements include a ^{1}/$_4$" seam allowance.*

BLOCK A
From cream print fabric:
- Cut 1 **background square** 10^1/$_2$" x 10^1/$_2$".

From white solid fabric:
- Cut 4 **rectangle B's** 1^3/$_4$" x ^{7}/$_8$".
- Cut 4 **rectangle E's** 2^5/$_8$" x ^{7}/$_8$".

From red polka dot fabric:
- Cut 4 **rectangle A's** 1^3/$_4$" x ^{7}/$_8$".
- Cut 4 **rectangle D's** 2^5/$_8$" x ^{7}/$_8$".
- Cut 1 **small heart** from pattern.

From blue print fabric:
- Cut 4 **rectangle C's** 1^3/$_8$" x 1^1/$_4$".

From brown print fabric:
- Cut 4 **flagpoles** ^{1}/$_2$" x 4^3/$_8$" for appliqué.

From green print fabric:
- Cut 4 **large leaves** and 4 **large leaves in reverse** from pattern.
- Cut 4 **small leaves** and 4 **small leaves in reverse** from pattern.

BLOCK B
From white solid fabric:
- Cut 1 **background rectangle** 10^1/$_2$" x 5^1/$_2$".
- Cut 3 **strips** 1^1/$_2$" x 11".

From red print fabric:
- Cut 3 **strips** $1^1/2$" x 11".

From blue and red striped fabric:
- Cut 4 **squares** $2^3/4$" x $2^3/4$".

From red and white striped fabric:
- Cut 4 **squares** $2^3/4$" x $2^3/4$".

MAKING SECTION 8

*Follow **Piecing**, page 99, **Pressing**, page 100, and* *Appliqué, page 101, to make **Section 8**.*

BLOCK A

Size (including seam allowance): $8^1/2$" x $8^1/2$"

1. Sew 1 **rectangle A** and 1 **rectangle B** together to make **Unit 1**. Make 4 **Unit 1's**.

Unit 1 (make 4)

2. Sew 1 **Unit 1** and 1 **rectangle C** together to make **Unit 2**. Make 4 **Unit 2's**.

Unit 2 (make 4)

3. Sew 1 **rectangle D** and 1 **rectangle E** together to make **Unit 3**. Make 4 **Unit 3's**.

Unit 3 (make 4)

4. Sew 1 **Unit 2** and 1 **Unit 3** together to make **Unit 4**. Make 4 **Unit 4's**. Cut 4 pieces of fusible web slightly smaller than **Unit 4** and apply web to back of each **Unit 4**. Trim **Unit 4's** $1/4$" on all sides (indicated by dashed line in **Fig. 1**) to make 4 **flags** ($2^1/8$" x $1^1/2$") for appliqué.

Unit 4 (make 4)

Fig. 1

Flag (make 4)

5. Arrange **flags**, **flagpoles** (overlapping flags by $1/8$"), **leaves** and **small heart** on **background square**. (**Note:** *Make sure appliqué design fits into an* $7^3/4$" x $7^3/4$" area.) Appliqué in place.

6. Making sure appliquéd design is centered, trim **background rectangle** to $8^1/2$" x $8^1/2$" to make **Block A**.

Block A

BLOCK B
Size (including seam allowance): $8^{1}/_{2}$" x $7^{1}/_{2}$"

1. Sew 2 blue and red striped **squares** and 2 red and white striped **squares** together to make **Unit 5**. Make 2 **Unit 5's**.

Unit 5 (make 2)

2. Trace **pieced heart** pattern, page 45, including dotted lines, onto fusible web *twice*. Apply web to back of each **Unit 5** aligning dotted lines with seam lines. Cut along traced solid lines to make 2 **pieced hearts** for appliqués.

Pieced Heart (make 2)

3. Spacing **pieced hearts** $^{3}/_{4}$" apart, appliqué **pieced hearts** on **background rectangle**.
4. Making sure hearts are centered, trim **background rectangle** to $8^{1}/_{2}$" x $3^{1}/_{2}$" to make **Unit 6**.

Unit 6

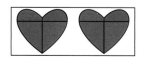

5. Sew 2 red **strips** and 1 white **strip** together to make **Strip Set A**. Cut across **Strip Set A** at $1^{1}/_{2}$" intervals to make 6 **Unit 7's**.

Strip Set A   **Unit 7** (make 6)

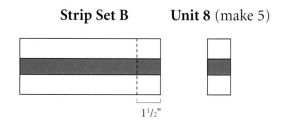

6. Sew 2 white **strips** and 1 red **strip** together to make **Strip Set B**. Cut across **Strip Set B** at $1^{1}/_{2}$" intervals to make 5 **Unit 8's**.

Strip Set B   **Unit 8** (make 5)

7. Sew 1 **Unit 7**, 1 **Unit 8**, then another **Unit 7** together; remove 1 red **square** from one end to make **Unit 9**.

Unit 9

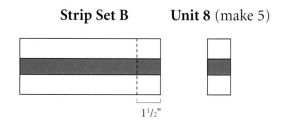

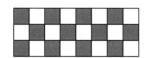

8. Sew 4 **Unit 7's** and 4 **Unit 8's** together to make **Unit 10**.

Unit 10

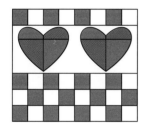

9. Sew **Unit 9**, **Unit 6**, and **Unit 10** together to make **Block B**.

Block B

Section 8

1. Sew **Block A** and **Block B** together to complete **Section 8**.

Section 8

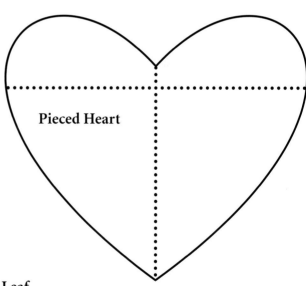

Small Leaf

Small Heart

Large Leaf

Pieced Heart

SECTION 9

Size (including seam allowance): 12$\frac{1}{2}$" x 15$\frac{1}{2}$"

YARDAGE REQUIREMENTS
BLOCK A
12" x 12" (30 cm x 30 cm) piece *each* of 3 gold print fabrics

9" x 22" (23 cm x 56 cm) piece of cream print fabric

BLOCK B
10" x 10" (25 cm x 25 cm) piece of light blue print fabric

10" x 4" (25 cm x 10 cm) piece of medium blue print fabric

Scraps of red, yellow, and royal blue print fabrics

BLOCK C's
10" x 8" (25 cm x 20 cm) piece of white solid fabric

6" x 5" (15 cm x 13 cm) piece of pink print fabric

6" x 5" (15 cm x 13 cm) piece of cream print fabric

6" x 5" (15 cm x 13 cm) piece of yellow print fabric

6" x 5" (15 cm x 13 cm) piece of green print fabric

6" x 3" (15 cm x 8 cm) piece of blue print fabric

BLOCK D
10" x 9" (25 cm x 23 cm) piece of light blue print fabric

12" x 8" (30 cm x 20 cm) piece of white solid fabric

5" x 5" (13 cm x 13 cm) piece of medium yellow print fabric

Scraps of red print, light yellow solid and dark yellow print

You will also need:
Paper-backed fusible web
Stabilizer

CUTTING OUT THE PIECES
*Refer to **Preparing Fusible Appliqué Pieces**, page 101, and use patterns on pages 52 – 53 to cut appliqué pieces. Follow **Template Cutting**, page 99, to make templates from patterns **A – C** on page 51. Background pieces are cut larger than needed and will be trimmed after appliqués are added. All other measurements include a $\frac{1}{4}$" seam allowance.*

BLOCK B

From light blue print fabric:
- Cut 1 **background square** 8$\frac{1}{2}$" x 8$\frac{1}{2}$".

From medium blue print fabric:
- Cut 1 **ocean** from pattern.

From red print fabric:
- Cut 1 **boat** from pattern.
- Cut 1 **mast** from pattern.

From yellow print fabric:
- Cut 1 **sail #1** from pattern.
- Cut 1 **sail #2** from pattern.

From royal blue print fabric:
- Cut 1 **flag** from pattern.

BLOCK C

From white solid fabric:
- Cut 2 **C's** from template.

From pink print fabric:
- Cut 2 **A's** from template.

From cream print fabric:
- Cut 2 **A's** from template.

From yellow print fabric:
- Cut 2 **A's** from template.

From green print fabric:
- Cut 2 **A's** from template.

From blue print fabric:
- Cut 2 **B's** from template.

BLOCK D

From light blue print fabric:
- Cut 1 **background rectangle** $8^1/2$" x $7^1/2$".

From white solid fabric:
- Cut 3 **squares** $1^1/2$" x $1^1/2$".
- Cut 1 **pitcher** from pattern.
- Cut 1 **handle** from pattern.

From medium yellow print fabric:
- Cut 1 **lemonade** from pattern.

From red print fabric:
- Cut 3 **squares** $1^1/2$" x $1^1/2$".

From light yellow solid fabric:
- Cut 1 **large lemon pulp** from pattern.
- Cut 1 **small lemon pulp** from pattern.

From dark yellow print fabric:
- Cut 1 **large lemon rind** from pattern.
- Cut 1 **small lemon rind** from pattern.
- Cut 4 **large lemon segments** from pattern.
- Cut 2 **small lemon segments** from pattern.

MAKING SECTION 9

*Follow **Piecing**, page 99, **Pressing**, page 100, and **Appliqué**, page 101, to make **Section 9**.*

BLOCK A

Size (including seam allowance): $12^1/2$" x $3^1/2$"

Note: *You will make 6 paper-pieced **Star Units**. Make 2 **Star Units** using each gold print (2 of these **Star Units** will be used in **Section 14**).*

1. For paper piecing foundations, use a fine-point marker and ruler to trace **Unit 1** pattern on page 50 onto paper. Make 6 traced patterns; cut out.

2. Rough cut a piece of cream print fabric at least $1/2$" larger on all sides than area 1 on the traced pattern (foundation).

3. Place fabric piece right side down; place foundation, traced side up, on top of fabric piece making sure fabric extends at least $1/2$" beyond all sides of area 1. Pin or glue fabric in place (**Fig. 1**).

Fig. 1

4. Rough cut a piece of gold fabric at least $1/2$" larger on all sides than area 2. Turning foundation and fabric #1 over so that traced side of foundation is facing down, place fabric #2 on fabric #1, matching right sides. Pin fabric pieces in place (**Fig. 2**).

Fig. 2

5. Turn foundation and fabric pieces over so that traced side of foundation is facing up; sew along line between areas 1 and 2, sewing a few stitches beyond beginning and end of line (**Fig. 3**).

Fig. 3

6. Fold back area 2 of foundation at stitching line and using ruler and rotary cutter, trim fabric pieces ¹/₄" from seam (**Fig. 4**).

Fig. 4

7. Unfold foundation, and turn foundation and fabric pieces over so that traced side of foundation is facing down. Open out piece #2; press (**Fig. 5**).

Fig. 5

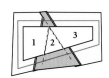

8. Continue in the same manner to cover area 3 with a piece of cream fabric. Using ruler and rotary cutter, trim fabric ¹/₄" from outer edges of foundation as indicated by red line in **Fig. 6**. Carefully tear away foundation paper to make **Unit 1**. Make 6 **Unit 1's**.

Fig. 6

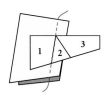

Unit 1 (make 6)

9. Follow Steps 1 – 8 to make 6 **Unit 2's** from **Unit 2** pattern.

Unit 2 (make 6)

10. Follow Steps 1 – 8 to make 6 **Unit 3's** from **Unit 3** pattern.

Unit 3 (make 6)

11. Using matching prints, sew **Unit 1**, **Unit 2**, then **Unit 3** together to make **Star Unit**. Make 6 **Star Units**. (*Set aside 2 Star Units for Section 14*).

Star Unit (make 6)

12. Sew 4 **Star Units** together to make **Block A**.

Block A

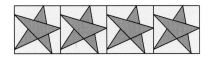

BLOCK B

Size (including seam allowance): 6¹/₂" x 6¹/₂"

1. Matching side and bottom raw edges of **ocean** appliqué piece and **background square**, arrange **ocean**, **boat**, **mast**, **sails**, and **flag** onto **background square**; appliqué in place.
2. Referring to photo, page 46, and **Block B** diagram for placement, trim **background square** to 6¹/₂" x 6¹/₂" to make **Block B**.

Block B

BLOCK C's

Size (including seam allowance): 6¹/₂" x 6¹/₂"

1. Matching raw edges and dots, sew 1 pink print **A**, 1 yellow print **A**, 1 green print **A**, and 1 cream print **A** together to make **Unit 4**. Make 2 **Unit 4's**.

Unit 4 (make 2)

2. Matching raw edges and dots and clipping seam allowance as necessary, sew 1 **Unit 4** and 1 **B** together to make **Unit 5**. Make 2 **Unit 5's**.

Unit 5 (make 2)

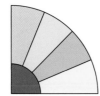

3. Matching raw edges and dots and clipping seam allowance as necessary, sew 1 **Unit 5** and 1 **C** together to make **Block C**. Make 2 **Block C's**.

Block C (make 2)

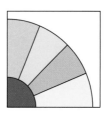

BLOCK D

Size (including seam allowance): 6¹/₂" x 6¹/₂"

1. Arrange **pitcher**, **handle**, **lemonade**, **lemon rinds**, **lemon pulps**, and **lemon segments** onto **background rectangle**; appliqué in place.
2. Making sure appliquéd design is centered, trim **background square** to 6¹/₂" x 5¹/₂" to make **Unit 6**.

Unit 6

3. Sew 3 red print **squares** and 3 white solid **squares** together to make **Unit 7**.

Unit 7

4. Sew **Unit 6** and **Unit 7** together to complete **Block D**.

Block D

SECTION 9

1. Sew **Block B** and 1 **Block C** together to make **Unit 8.**

Unit 8

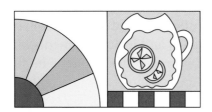

2. Sew 1 **Block C** and **Block D** together to make **Unit 9.**

Unit 9

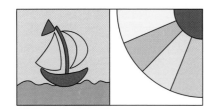

3. Sew **Block A**, **Unit 8**, and **Unit 9** together to complete **Section 9.**

Section 9

Unit 1 Paper Piecing Pattern

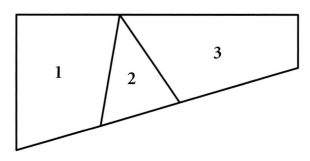

Unit 2 Paper Piecing Pattern

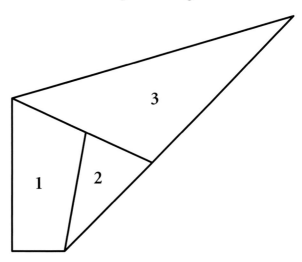

Unit 3 Paper Piecing Pattern

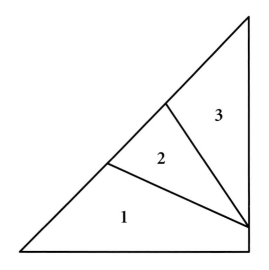

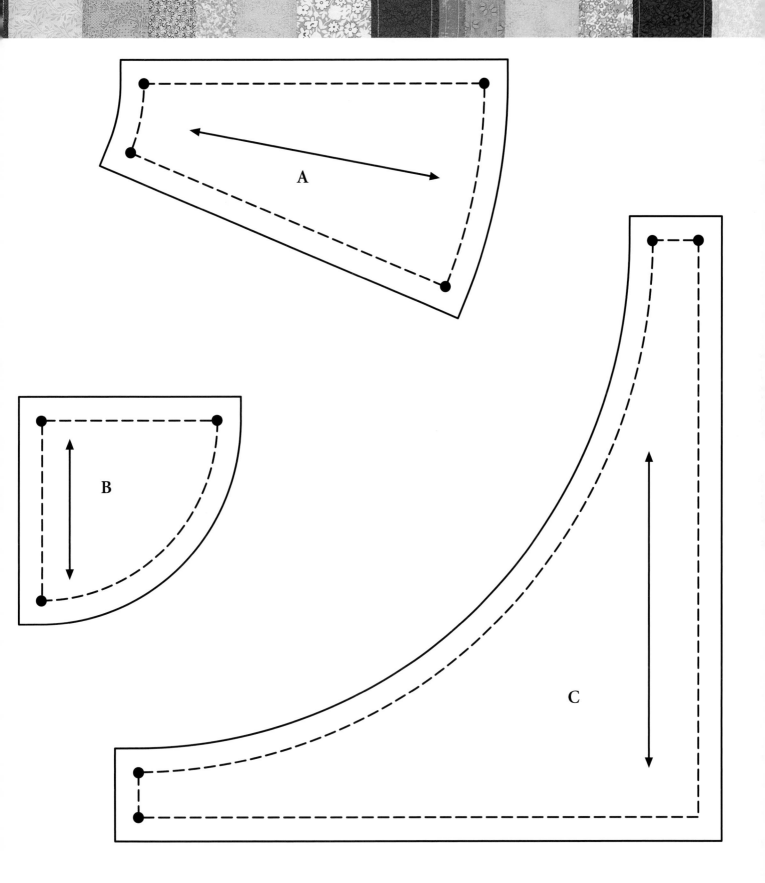

A

B

C

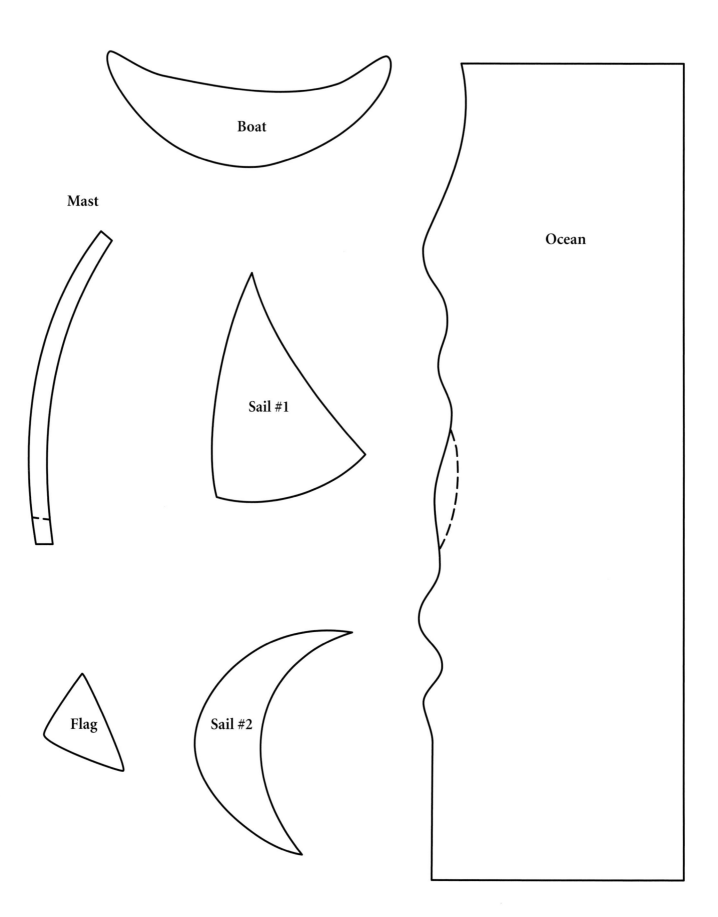

Boat

Mast

Ocean

Sail #1

Flag

Sail #2

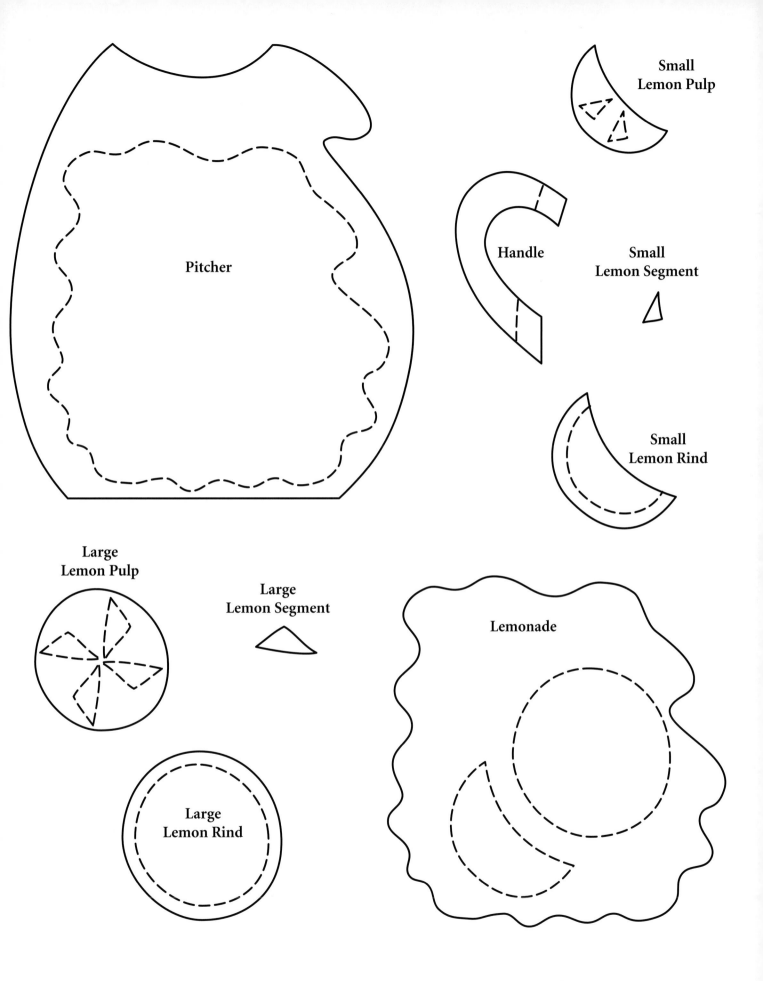

Pitcher

Small Lemon Pulp

Handle

Small Lemon Segment

Small Lemon Rind

Large Lemon Pulp

Large Lemon Segment

Lemonade

Large Lemon Rind

SECTION 10

Size (including seam allowance): 12¹/₂" x 15¹/₂"

YARDAGE REQUIREMENTS
BLOCK A
10" x 10" (25 cm x 25 cm) piece of green checked fabric

9" x 22" (23 cm x 56 cm) piece of cream print fabric

10" x 10" (25 cm x 25 cm) piece of dark green print fabric

Scrap of brown print fabric

BLOCK B
6" x 11" (15 cm x 28 cm) piece of white solid fabric

6" x11" (15 cm x 28 cm) piece of royal blue print fabric

CUTTING OUT THE PIECES
All measurements include a ¹/₄" seam allowance.

BLOCK A
From green checked fabric:
- Cut 9 **large squares** 2⁷/₈" x 2⁷/₈".

From cream print fabric:
- Cut 1 square 8¹/₂" x 8¹/₂". Cut square *twice* diagonally to make 4 **small triangles**. (You will use 2 and have 2 left over.)
- Cut 9 **large squares** 2⁷/₈" x 2⁷/₈".
- Cut 2 **small squares** 2¹/₂" x 2¹/₂".

From dark green print fabric:
- Cut 1 square 8⁷/₈" x 8⁷/₈". Cut square *once* diagonally to make 2 **large triangles**. (You will use 1 and have 1 left over.)

From brown print fabric:
- Cut 1 **rectangle** 6¹/₂" x 1¹/₂".

BLOCK B
From white solid fabric:
- Cut 8 **squares** 2³/₈" x 2³/₈".

From royal blue print fabric:
- Cut 8 **squares** 2³/₈" x 2³/₈".

MAKING SECTION 10

*Follow **Piecing**, page 99, and **Pressing**, page 100, to make Section 10.*

BLOCK A

Size (including seam allowance): 12¹/₂" x 12¹/₂"

1. Sew 2 **small triangles** and **rectangle** together to make **Unit 1**. Trim **rectangle** even with triangles as shown.

Unit 1

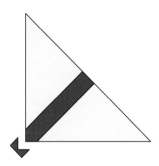

2. Sew **Unit 1** and 1 **large triangle** together to make **Unit 2**.

Unit 2

3. Draw diagonal line (corner to corner) on wrong side of each cream **large square**. With right sides together, place 1 cream **large square** on top of 1 green **large square**. Stitch seam ¹/₄" from each side of drawn line (**Fig. 1**).

Fig. 1

4. Cut along drawn line and press open to make 2 **Large Triangle-Squares**. Repeat with remaining **large squares** to make 18 **Large Triangle-Squares**.

Large Triangle-Squares (make 18)

5. Sew 4 **Large Triangle-Squares** together to make **Unit 3**.

Unit 3

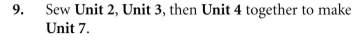

6. Sew 4 **Large Triangle-Squares** and 1 **small square** together to make **Unit 4**.

Unit 4

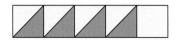

7. Sew 5 **Large Triangle-Squares** together to make **Unit 5**.

Unit 5

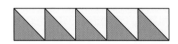

8. Sew 5 **Large Triangle-Squares** and 1 **small square** together to make **Unit 6**.

Unit 6

9. Sew **Unit 2**, **Unit 3**, then **Unit 4** together to make **Unit 7**.

Unit 7

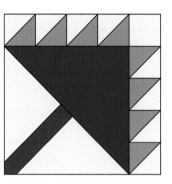

10. Sew **Unit 7**, **Unit 5**, then **Unit 6** together to make **Block A**.

Block A

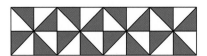

BLOCK B
Size (including seam allowance): 12$\frac{1}{2}$" x 3$\frac{1}{2}$"

1. Draw diagonal line (corner to corner) on wrong side of each white **square**. With right sides together, place 1 white **square** on top of 1 royal blue **square**. Stitch seam $\frac{1}{4}$" from each side of drawn line (**Fig. 2**).

Fig. 2

2. Cut along drawn line and press open to make 2 **Small Triangle-Squares**. Repeat with remaining **squares** to make 16 **Small Triangle-Squares**.

Small Triangle-Squares (make 16)

3. Sew 4 **Small Triangle-Squares** together to make **Unit 8**. Make 4 **Unit 8's**.

Unit 8 (make 4)

4. Sew 4 **Unit 8's** together to make **Block B**.

Block B

5. SECTION 10
1. Sew **Block A** and **Block B** together to complete **Section 10**.

Section 10

57

SECTION 11

Size (including seam allowance): $12^{1}/_{2}$" x $15^{1}/_{2}$"

YARDAGE REQUIREMENTS
BLOCK A
14" x 14" (36 cm x 36 cm) piece of cream solid fabric
6" x 6" (15 cm x 15 cm) piece of light pink solid fabric
10" x 8" (25 cm x 20 cm) piece of light blue print fabric
6" x 4" (15 cm x 10 cm) piece of red polka dot fabric
5" x 3" (13 cm x 8 cm) piece of dark blue print fabric
BLOCK B
13" x 10" (33 cm x 25 cm) piece of cream print fabric
10" x 10" (25 cm x 25 cm) piece of brown print fabric
8" x 6" (20 cm x 15 cm) piece of medium red print fabric
6" x 4" (15 cm x 10 cm) piece of dark red print fabric
Scrap of gold print fabric
BLOCK C
8" x 13" (20 cm x 33 cm) piece of light blue print fabric
5" x 8" (13 cm x 20 cm) piece of green print fabric
Scrap of brown print fabric
BLOCK D
16" x 6" (41 cm x 15 cm) piece of yellow print fabric
6" x 6" (15 cm x 15 cm) piece of red print fabric
Scrap of green print fabric
You will also need:
Gold size #3 pearl cotton
Black and gold embroidery floss
Paper-backed fusible web
Stabilizer
Lightweight copy paper or typing paper

CUTTING OUT THE PIECES
*Refer to **Preparing Fusible Appliqué Pieces**, page 101, and use patterns on page 64 to cut appliqué pieces. Follow **Template Cutting**, page 99, to make templates from patterns A and B on page 65. Background pieces for **Blocks C** and **D** are cut larger than needed and will be trimmed after appliqués are added. All other measurements include a $^{1}/_{4}$" seam allowance.*

BLOCK A
From cream solid fabric:
- Cut 4 **rectangle A's** $3^{1}/_{2}$" x $1^{3}/_{4}$".
- Cut 4 **square D's** $1^{1}/_{2}$" x $1^{1}/_{2}$".
- Cut 2 **rectangle F's** $^{3}/_{4}$" x $1^{1}/_{2}$".
- Cut 4 **rectangle G's** $1^{1}/_{2}$" x $1^{1}/_{4}$".
- Cut 4 **rectangle H's** $1^{1}/_{2}$" x 2".
- Cut 2 **rectangle J's** $^{3}/_{4}$" x 2".

From light pink solid fabric:
- Cut 8 **square C's** 1" x 1".
- Cut 4 **rectangle E's** $^{7}/_{8}$" x $1^{1}/_{2}$".
- Cut 4 **heads** from pattern.

From light blue print fabric:
- Cut 2 **rectangle B's** $2^{1}/_{2}$" x 1".

From red polka dot fabric:
- Cut 2 **rectangle B's** $2^{1}/_{2}$" x 1".
- Cut 2 **rectangle G's** $1^{1}/_{2}$" x $1^{1}/_{4}$".

From dark blue print fabric:
- Cut 4 **rectangle I's** $^{7}/_{8}$" x 2".

Reserve remaining cream solid and light blue print fabrics for paper piecing.

BLOCK B

From cream print fabric:

- Cut 1 **square** $1^1/_2$" x $1^1/_2$".
- Cut 4 **large rectangles** $4^1/_2$" x $1^1/_2$".
- Cut 2 **medium rectangles** $3^3/_4$" x $1^1/_2$".
- Cut 1 **A** and 1 **A in reverse** from template.

From brown print fabric:

- Cut 2 **squares** $1^1/_2$" x $1^1/_2$".
- Cut 2 **small rectangles** $^3/_4$" x $1^1/_2$".
- Cut 1 **B** from template.

From medium red print fabric:

- Cut 1 **largest rectangle** $6^1/_2$" x $4^1/_2$".

From dark red print fabric:

- Cut 1 **door** $1^1/_2$" x 2" for appliqué.
- Cut 5 **windows** 1" x 1" for appliqué.

From gold print fabric:

- Cut 1 **bell** from pattern.

BLOCK C

From light blue print fabric:

- Cut 1 **background rectangle** $6^1/_2$" x $11^1/_2$".

From green print fabric:

- Cut 1 **tree** from pattern.

From brown print fabric:

- Cut 1 **trunk** from pattern.

BLOCK D

From yellow print fabric:

- Cut 1 **background rectangle** $14^1/_2$" x $4^1/_2$".

From red print fabric:

- Cut 4 **apples** from pattern.

From green print fabric:

- Cut 4 **leaves** from pattern.

MAKING SECTION 11

Follow **Piecing**, *page 99,* **Pressing**, *page 100, and* **Appliqué**, *page 101, to make* **Section 11**.

BLOCK A

Size (including seam allowance): $12^1/_2$" x $4^1/_2$"

1. For paper piecing foundations, use a fine-point marker and ruler to trace **Unit 1** pattern on page 64 onto paper. Make 2 traced patterns; cut out.

2. Rough cut a piece of light blue print fabric at least $^1/_2$" larger on all sides than area 1 on the traced pattern (foundation).

3. Place fabric piece right side down; place foundation with traced side facing up on top of fabric piece making sure fabric extends at least $^1/_2$" beyond all sides of area 1. Pin or glue fabric in place (**Fig. 1**).

Fig. 1

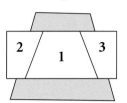

4. Rough cut a piece of cream fabric at least $^1/_2$" larger on all sides than area 2. Turning foundation and fabric #1 over so that traced side of foundation is facing down, place fabric #2 on fabric #1, matching right sides. Pin fabric pieces in place (**Fig. 2**).

Fig. 2

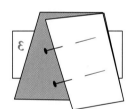

5. Turn foundation and fabric pieces over so that traced side of foundation is facing up; sew along line between areas 1 and 2, sewing a few stitches beyond beginning and end of line (**Fig. 3**).

Fig. 3

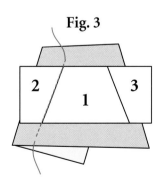

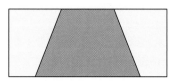

6. Fold back area 2 of foundation at stitching line and using ruler and rotary cutter, trim fabric pieces ¹/₄" from seam (**Fig. 4**).

Fig. 4

7. Unfold foundation, and turn foundation and fabric pieces over so that traced side of foundation is facing down. Open out piece #2; press (**Fig. 5**).

Fig. 5

8. Continue in the same manner to cover area 3 with a piece of cream fabric. Using ruler and rotary cutter, trim fabric ¹/₄" from outer edges of foundation as indicated by red line in **Fig. 6**. Carefully tear away foundation paper to make **Unit 1**. Make 2 **Unit 1's**.

Fig. 6

Unit 1 (make 2)

9. Sew 2 **square C's** and 1 light blue **rectangle B** together to make **Unit 2**. Make 2 **Unit 2's**.

Unit 2 (make 2)

10. Sew 2 **square D's**, 2 **rectangle E's**, and 1 **rectangle F** together to make **Unit 3**. Make 2 **Unit 3's**.

Unit 3 (make 2)

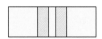

11. Sew 1 **rectangle A**, 1 **Unit 2**, 1 **Unit 1**, and 1 **Unit 3** together to make **Unit 4**. Make 2 **Unit 4's**.

Unit 4 (make 2)

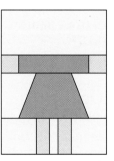

12. Sew 2 **square C's** and 1 red **rectangle B** together to make **Unit 5**. Make 2 **Unit 5's**.

Unit 5 (make 2)

13. Sew 2 cream **rectangle G's** and 1 red **rectangle G** together to make **Unit 6**. Make 2 **Unit 6's**.

Unit 6 (make 2)

14. Sew 2 **rectangle H's**, 2 **rectangle I's**, and 1 **rectangle J** together to make **Unit 7**. Make 2 **Unit 7's**.

Unit 7 (make 2)

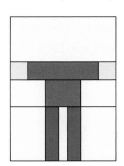

15. Sew 1 **rectangle A**, 1 **Unit 5**, 1 **Unit 6**, and 1 **Unit 7** together to make **Unit 8**. Make 2 **Unit 8's**.

Unit 8 (make 2)

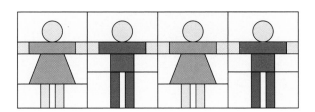

16. Sew 2 **Unit 4's** and 2 **Unit 8's** together to make **Unit 9**. Appliqué 1 **head** on each child as shown.

Unit 9

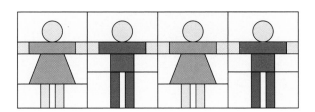

17. Using 2 strands of black floss, make Straight Stitches for eyes and mouths. Referring to photos below, Couch Stitch desired number and length of strands of gold pearl cotton with 1 strand of gold floss around top of head, making loops, braiding strands, or fraying ends as desired to make hair for each child. (Couch Stitch is shown on page 110.)

Block A

BLOCK B

Size (including seam allowance): $8^1/_2$" x $9^1/_2$"

1. With right sides together, place 1 brown **square** on top of 1 **large rectangle** and stitch diagonally. Trim $^1/_4$" from seam; press open to make **Unit 10a**. Make 1 **Unit 10a** and 1 **Unit 10b**.

Unit 10a

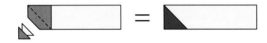

Unit 10b

2. Sew **Unit 10a** and **Unit 10b** together to make **Unit 11**.

Unit 11

3. Sew 2 **medium rectangles**, 2 **small rectangles**, and 1 cream **square** together to make **Unit 12**.

Unit 12

4. Sew 1 **A**, 1 **B**, and 1 **A reversed** together to make **Unit 13**.

Unit 13

5. Sew 2 **large rectangles** and 1 **largest rectangle** together to make **Unit 14**.

Unit 14

6. Sew **Unit 11**, **Unit 12**, **Unit 13**, and **Unit 14** together to make **Unit 15**.

Unit 15

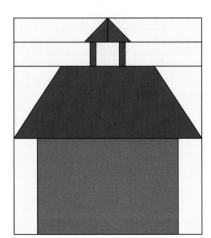

7. Centering **door** horizontally and matching bottom edges of **door** and **Unit 15**, arrange **door**, **windows**, and **bell**; appliqué. Add machine Satin Stitch detail to clapper of **bell**. Using 3 strands of black floss, Stem Stitch panes in **windows** to make **Block B**.

Block B

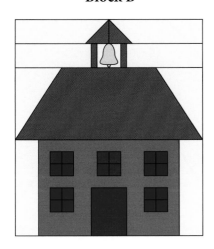

BLOCK C
Size (including seam allowance): $4^1/2$" x $9^1/2$"

1. Arrange and appliqué **trunk** and **tree** onto **background rectangle**.
2. Making sure appliquéd design is centered, trim **background rectangle** to $4^1/2$" x $9^1/2$" to make **Block C**.

Block C

BLOCK D
Size (including seam allowance): $12^1/2$" x $2^1/2$"

1. Leaving a $1^3/8$" space between **apples**, align **apples** horizontally onto **background rectangle**. Appliqué **apples** and **leaves**. Machine Satin Stitch vein details in leaves.
2. Making sure appliquéd design is centered, trim **background rectangle** to $12^1/2$" x $2^1/2$" to make **Block D**.

Block D

SECTION 11

1. Sew **Block B** and **Block C** together. Add **Block A**, then **Block D** to complete **Section 11**.

Section 11

Unit 1 Paper Piecing Pattern

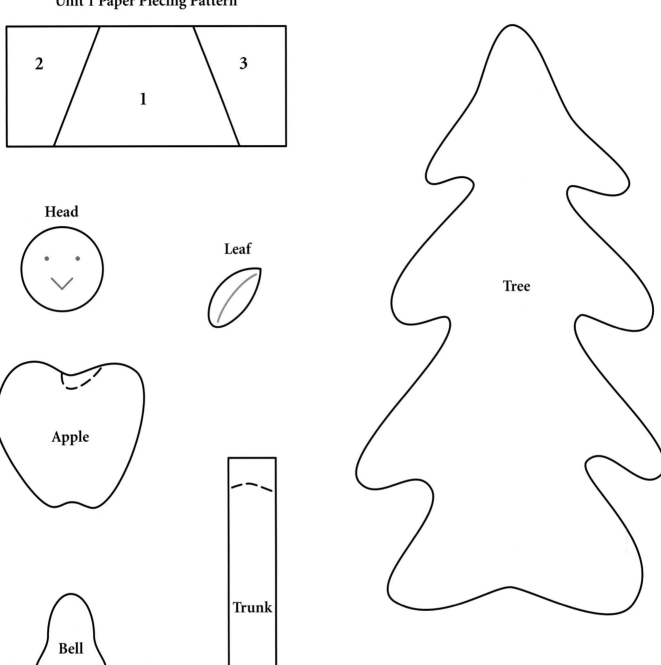

2

1

3

Head

Leaf

Apple

Trunk

Bell

Tree

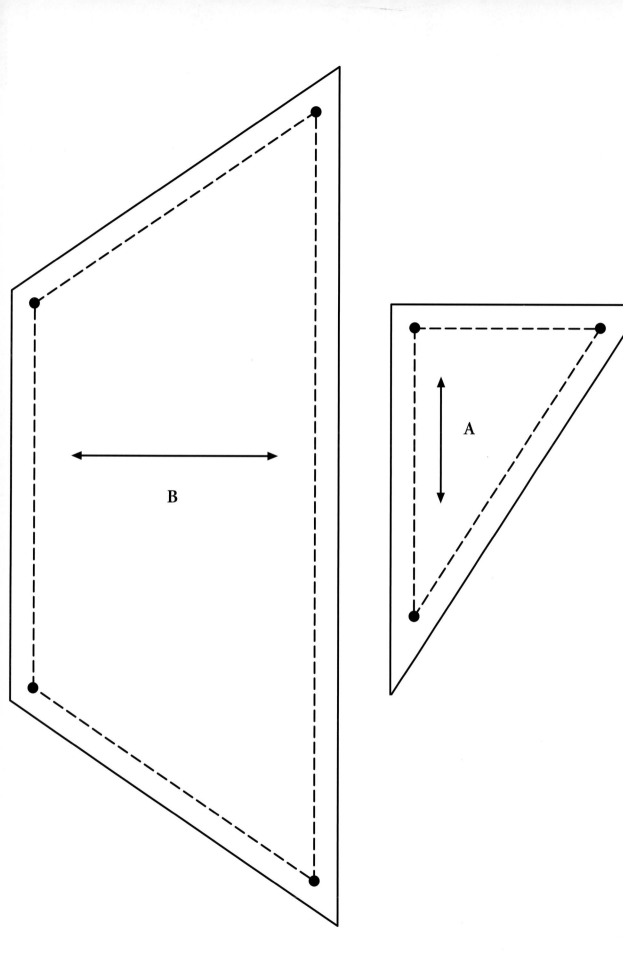

SECTION 12

Size (including seam allowance): 12¹/₂" x 15¹/₂"

YARDAGE REQUIREMENTS
BLOCK A
  13" x 13" (33 cm x 33 cm) piece of cream print fabric
  4" x 4" (10 cm x 10 cm) piece *each* of 4 different
    gold print fabrics
BLOCK B
  13" x 13" (33 cm x 33 cm) piece of tan checked fabric
  9" x 22" (23 cm x 56 cm) piece of tan and red print
    fabric
  8" x 16" (20 cm x 41 cm) piece of tan print fabric
  4" x 16" (10 cm x 41 cm) piece of rust print fabric
  4" x 6" (10 cm x 15 cm) piece of orange print
    fabric #1
  4" x 4" (10 cm x 10 cm) piece *each* of orange print
    fabric #2 and orange print fabric #3
  6" x 4" (15 cm x 10 cm) piece of black solid fabric
  Scrap of brown print fabric
You will also need:
  Gold embroidery floss
  Paper-backed fusible web
  Stabilizer

CUTTING OUT THE PIECES
*Refer to **Preparing Fusible Appliqué Pieces**, page 101, and
use patterns on pages 69 – 70 to cut appliqué pieces. The
background pieces are cut larger than needed and will be
trimmed after appliqués are added. All other measurements
include a ¹/₄" seam allowance.*
BLOCK A
From cream print fabric:
  • Cut 4 **background squares** 5¹/₂" x 5¹/₂".
From *each* gold print fabric:
  • Cut 1 **wheat sheaf** from pattern for a total of
    4 **sheaves**.

BLOCK B
From tan checked fabric:
  • Cut 1 **background square** 11" x 11".
From tan and red print fabric:
  • Cut 4 **squares** 3³/₈" x 3³/₈".
  • Cut 4 squares 3⁷/₈" x 3⁷/₈". Cut squares *once*
    diagonally to make 8 **triangles**.
From tan print fabric:
  • Cut 2 **long strips** 1¹/₂" x 14".
  • Cut 2 **short strips** 1¹/₂" x 8".
From rust print fabric:
  • Cut 1 **long strip** 1¹/₂" x 14".
  • Cut 1 **short strip** 1¹/₂" x 8".
From orange print fabric #1:
  • Cut 1 **tall pumpkin** from pattern.

From orange print fabric #2:
- Cut 1 **medium pumpkin** from pattern.

From orange print fabric #3:
- Cut 1 **small pumpkin** from pattern.

From black solid fabric:
- Cut 1 **tall pumpkin face** (2 eyes, 1 nose, and 1 mouth) from patterns.
- Cut 1 **medium pumpkin face** (2 eyes and 1 mouth) from patterns.
- Cut 1 **small pumpkin face** (2 eyes and 1 mouth) from patterns.

From brown print fabric:
- Cut 1 *each* of **tall pumpkin stem**, **medium pumpkin stem**, and **small pumpkin stem**.

MAKING SECTION 12

*Follow **Piecing**, page 99, **Pressing**, page 100, and **Appliqué**, page 101, to make **Section 12**.*

BLOCK A

Size (including seam allowance): 12$^1/_2$" x 3$^1/_2$"

1. Appliqué 1 **wheat sheaf** onto 1 **background square**. Stem Stitch ropes using 6 strands of gold floss.
2. Making sure appliquéd design is centered, trim **background square** to 3$^1/_2$" x 3$^1/_2$" to make **Unit 1**. Make 4 **Unit 1's**.

Unit 1 (make 4)

3. Sew 4 **Unit 1's** together to make **Block A**.

Block A

BLOCK B

Size (including seam allowance): 12$^1/_2$" x 12$^1/_2$"

1. Turning background square diagonally, arrange **stems**, **pumpkins**, and **faces** on **background square**. (***Note:** Make sure entire appliqué design is no wider than 6$^3/_4$".*) Appliqué pieces in place (**Fig. 1**).

Fig. 1

2. Turn **background square** so that appliquéd design is at a 45° angle. Referring to **Unit 2** diagram and making sure appliquéd design is $^3/_4$" from right edge and $^3/_4$" from bottom edge of **background square**, trim **background square** to 9" x 9" to make **Unit 2**.

Unit 2

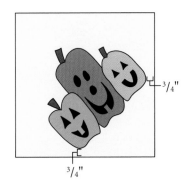

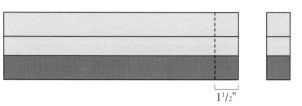

3. With right sides together, place 1 **square** on 1 corner of **Unit 2** and stitch diagonally. Trim ¹/₄" from stitching line (**Fig. 2**).

Fig. 2

4. Open up and press, pressing seam allowances to darker fabric. Repeat to add **squares** to each corner to make **Unit 3**.

Unit 3

5. Sew 2 tan print **long strips** and 1 rust print **long strip** together to make **Strip Set A**. Cut across **Strip Set A** at 1¹/₂" intervals to make 8 **Unit 4's**.

Strip Set A　　　　**Unit 4** (make 8)

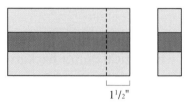

1¹/₂"

6. Sew 2 tan print **short strips** and 1 rust print **short strip** together to make **Strip Set B**. Cut across **Strip Set B** at 1¹/₂" intervals to make 4 **Unit 5's**.

Strip Set B　　**Unit 5** (make 4)

1¹/₂"

7. Sew 2 **Unit 4's** and 1 **Unit 5** together to make **Unit 6**. Make 4 **Unit 6's**.

Unit 6 (make 4)

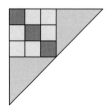

8. Sew 1 **Unit 6** and 2 **triangles** together to make **Unit 7**. Make 4 **Unit 7's**.

Unit 7 (make 4)

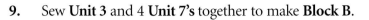

9. Sew **Unit 3** and 4 **Unit 7's** together to make **Block B**.

Block B

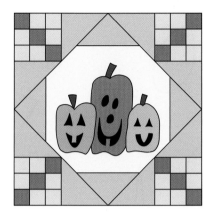

Wheat Sheaf

SECTION 12

1. Sew **Block A** and **Block B** together to complete **Section 12**.

Section 12

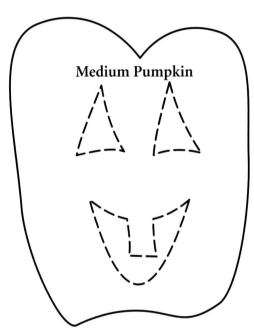

Medium Pumpkin

Medium Pumpkin Face

Medium Pumpkin Stem

69

Tall Pumpkin

Tall Pumpkin Face

Tall Pumpkin Stem

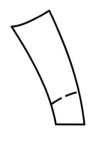

Small Pumpkin Face

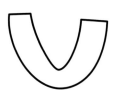

Small Pumpkin

Small Pumpkin Stem

SECTION 13

Size (including seam allowance): 13¹/2" x 15¹/2"

YARDAGE REQUIREMENTS
BLOCK A
- 6" x 11" (15 cm x 28) piece of tan print fabric
- 6" x 11" (15 cm x 28) piece of blue print fabric
- 5" x 9" (13 cm x 23) piece of blue plaid fabric

BLOCK B
- 14" x 13" (36 cm x 33 cm) piece of cream print fabric
- 7" x 5" (18 cm x 13 cm) piece *each* of tan print, rust print, blue print, light green print, and tan and black polka dot fabrics
- 5" x 5" (13 cm x 13 cm) piece *each* of 3 brown print fabrics
- 5" x 4" (13 cm x 10 cm) piece of dark green print fabric

You will also need:
- Paper-backed fusible web
- Stabilizer

CUTTING OUT THE PIECES

*Refer to **Preparing Fusible Appliqué Pieces**, page 101, and use patterns on page 74 to cut appliqué pieces. The background rectangle for **Block B** is cut larger than needed and will be trimmed after appliqués are added. All other measurements include a 1/4" seam allowance.*

BLOCK A
From tan print fabric:
- Cut 2 **large squares** 4¹/4" x 4¹/4".

From blue print fabric:
- Cut 2 **large squares** 4¹/4" x 4¹/4".

From blue plaid fabric:
- Cut 2 **small squares** 3¹/2" x 3¹/2".

BLOCK B
From cream print fabric:
- Cut 1 **background rectangle** 12¹/2" x 11¹/2".

From tan print fabric:
- Cut 2 **rectangles** 2¹/2" x 3¹/2".

From rust print fabric:
- Cut 2 **rectangles** 2¹/2" x 3¹/2".

From blue print fabric:
- Cut 2 **rectangles** 2¹/2" x 3¹/2".

From light green print fabric:
- Cut 2 **rectangles** 2¹/2" x 3¹/2".

From tan and black polka dot fabric:
- Cut 2 **rectangles** 2¹/2" x 3¹/2".

From *each* brown print fabric:
- Cut 2 **leaves** from pattern (for a total of 6 **leaves**).

From dark green print fabric:
- Cut 1 **bow** from pattern.

MAKING SECTION 13

*Follow **Piecing**, page 99, **Pressing**, page 100, and **Appliqué**, page 101, to make **Section 13**.*

BLOCK A

Size (including seam allowance): $3^1/2$" x $15^1/2$"

1. Draw diagonal lines from corner to corner in both directions on wrong side of each tan print **large square**. With right sides together, place 1 tan print **large square** on top of 1 blue print **large square**. Stitch seam $1/4$" from each side of 1 drawn line (**Fig. 1**).

Fig. 1

2. Cut along drawn line and press open to make 2 **Triangle-Squares**. Repeat with remaining **large squares** to make 4 **Triangle-Squares**.

Triangle-Squares (make 4)

3. On wrong side of 1 **Triangle-Square**, extend drawn line from corner of tan print triangle to corner of blue print triangle.

4. Match 2 **Triangle-Squares** with contrasting fabrics facing and marked unit on top. Stitch seam $1/4$" on each side of drawn line (**Fig. 2**). Cut apart along drawn line between stitching to make 2 **Hourglass Units**; press **Hourglass Units** open. Make 4 **Hourglass Units** (you will use 3 and have 1 left over).

Fig. 2

Hourglass Units (make 4)

5. Sew 3 **Hourglass Units** and 2 **small squares** together to make **Block A**.

Block A

BLOCK B
Size (including seam allowance): $10^1/2$" x $15^1/2$"

1. Sew **5 rectangles** (1 of each print and polka dot) together to make **Unit 1**. Make 2 **Unit 1's**.

Unit 1 (make 2)

2. Arrange **leaves** and **bow** onto **background rectangle**. *(Note: Make sure appliqué design fits into a $9^1/2$" x $8^1/2$" area.)* Appliqué pieces in place. Add machine Satin Stitch details to **leaves** and **bow**.

3. Making sure appliquéd design is centered, trim **background rectangle** to $10^1/2$" x $9^1/2$" to make **Unit 2**.

Unit 2

4. Sew **Unit 2** and 2 **Unit 1's** together to make **Block B**.

Block B

SECTION 13
1. Sew **Block A** and **Block B** together to complete **Section 13**.

Section 13

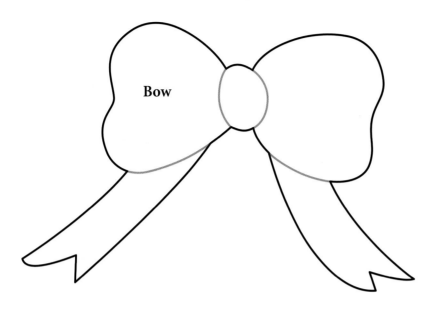

Bow

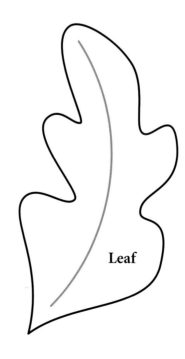

Leaf

SECTION 14

Size (including seam allowance): 19$^{1}/_{2}$" x 15$^{1}/_{2}$"

YARDAGE REQUIREMENTS

BLOCK A

- 15" x 15" (38 cm x 38 cm) piece of cream solid fabric
- 8" x 8" (20 cm x 20 cm) piece of gold print fabric

BLOCK B

- 9" x 22" (23 cm x 56 cm) piece of tan print fabric
- 5" x 5" (13 cm x 13 cm) piece of brown print fabric
- Scraps of white solid and red print fabrics
- 8" x 4" (20 cm x 10 cm) piece *each* of 3 green print fabrics

BLOCK C

- 9" x 22" (23 cm x 56 cm) piece of cream print fabric
- 12" x 10" (30 cm x 25 cm) piece of red and yellow print fabric
- 10" x 8" (25 cm x 20 cm) piece of green print fabric
- 5" x 5" (13 cm x 13 cm) piece of red print fabric
- Scraps of pink solid, tan print, and red and black print fabrics

BLOCK D

- Scraps of white solid and red print fabrics

BLOCK E

- 6" x 15" (15 cm x 38 cm) piece of white solid fabric
- 6" x 15" (15 cm x 38 cm) piece of red print fabric

You will also need:

- Rust and black embroidery floss
- Paper-backed fusible web
- Stabilizer

CUTTING OUT THE PIECES

Refer to **Preparing Fusible Appliqué Pieces***, page 101, and use patterns on page 83 to cut appliqué pieces. Follow* **Template Cutting***, page 99, to make templates from patterns A and B on page 83. All measurements include a* $^{1}/_{4}$" *seam allowance.*

BLOCK A

From cream solid fabric:

- Cut 4 **large squares** 3$^{1}/_{4}$" x 3$^{1}/_{4}$".
- Cut 10 **small squares** 2$^{1}/_{2}$" x 2$^{1}/_{2}$".

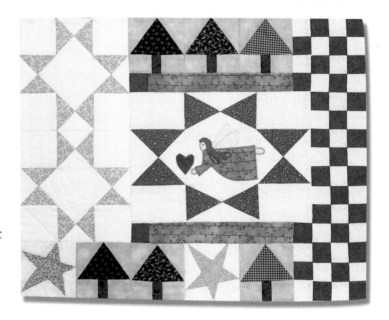

From gold print fabric:

- Cut 4 **large squares** 3$^{1}/_{4}$" x 3$^{1}/_{4}$".

BLOCK B

From tan print fabric:

- Cut 12 **large rectangles** 1$^{3}/_{4}$" x 1$^{1}/_{2}$".

From brown print fabric:

- Cut 6 **small rectangles** 1" x 1$^{1}/_{2}$".

From white solid fabric:

- Cut 2 **squares** 1$^{1}/_{2}$" x 1$^{1}/_{2}$".

From red print fabric:

- Cut 1 **square** 1$^{1}/_{2}$" x 1$^{1}/_{2}$".

Reserve green print and remaining tan print fabrics for paper piecing.

BLOCK C

From cream print fabric:

- Cut 1 **large square** 4$^{1}/_{4}$" x 4$^{1}/_{4}$".
- Cut 1 **large rectangle** 4$^{1}/_{2}$" x 3$^{1}/_{2}$".
- Cut 4 **small rectangles** 3$^{1}/_{2}$" x 2$^{1}/_{2}$".
- Cut 4 **A's** from template.

From red and yellow print fabric:

- Cut 1 **large square** 4$^{1}/_{4}$" x 4$^{1}/_{4}$".
- Cut 4 **B's** from template.

From green print fabric:

- Cut 2 **long rectangles** 8$^{1}/_{2}$" x 1$^{1}/_{2}$".
- Cut 1 **dress** from pattern.

From red print fabric:

- Cut 4 **small squares** 1$^{1}/_{2}$" x 1$^{1}/_{2}$".

From pink solid fabric:
- Cut 1 **head** from pattern.
- Cut 1 **hand** from pattern.
- Cut 1 **foot** from pattern.

From tan print fabric:
- Cut 1 **wings** from pattern.

From red and black print fabric:
- Cut 1 **heart** from pattern.

BLOCK D

From white solid fabric:
- Cut 2 **squares** $1^{1}/_{2}$" x $1^{1}/_{2}$".

From red print fabric:
- Cut 1 **square** $1^{1}/_{2}$" x $1^{1}/_{2}$".

BLOCK E

From white solid fabric:
- Cut 3 **strips** $1^{1}/_{2}$" x 14".

From red print fabric:
- Cut 3 **strips** $1^{1}/_{2}$" x 14".

MAKING SECTION 14

*Follow **Piecing**, page 99, **Pressing**, page 100, and **Appliqué**, page 101, to make **Section 14**.*

BLOCK A

Size (including seam allowance): $6^{1}/_{2}$" x $12^{1}/_{2}$"

1. Draw diagonal lines from corner to corner in both directions on wrong side of each cream **large square**. With right sides together, place 1 cream **large square** on top of 1 gold **large square**. Stitch seam $^{1}/_{4}$" from each side of 1 drawn line (**Fig. 1**).

Fig. 1

2. Cut along drawn line and press open to make 2 **Small Triangle-Squares**. Repeat with remaining **large squares** to make 8 **Small Triangle-Squares**.

Small Triangle-Squares (make 8)

3. On wrong side of 1 **Small Triangle-Square**, extend drawn line from corner of cream triangle to corner of gold triangle.

4. Match 2 **Small Triangle-Squares** with contrasting fabrics facing and marked unit on top. Stitch seam $^{1}/_{4}$" on each side of drawn line (**Fig. 2**). Cut apart along drawn line between stitching to make 2 **Small Hourglass Units**; press **Small Hourglass Units** open. Make 8 **Small Hourglass Units**.

Fig. 2

Small Hourglass Units (make 8)

5. Sew 2 **small squares** and 1 **Small Hourglass Unit** together to make **Unit 1**. Make 4 **Unit 1's**.

Unit 1 (make 4)

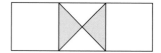

76

6. Sew 1 **small square** and 2 **Small Hourglass Unit's** together to make **Unit 2**. Make 2 **Unit 2's**.

Unit 2 (make 2)

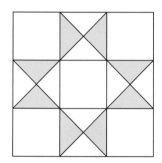

7. Sew 2 **Unit 1's** and 1 **Unit 2** together to make **Unit 3**. Make 2 **Unit 3's**.

Unit 3 (make 2)

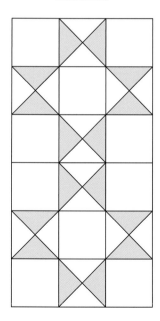

8. Sew 2 **Unit 3's** together to make **Block A**.

Block A

BLOCK B
Size (including seam allowance): 10½" x 3½"
*Note: You will make 6 **Tree Units**. Make 2 **Tree Units** using each green print. (3 **Tree Units** will be used in **Block D**.)*

1. To make paper piecing foundatons, use a fine-point marker and ruler to trace **Unit 4** pattern on page 83 onto paper. Make 6 traced patterns; cut out.

2. Rough cut a piece of green print fabric at least ½" larger on all sides than area 1 on the traced pattern (foundation).

3. Place fabric piece right side down; place foundation with traced side facing up on top of fabric piece making sure fabric extends at least ½" beyond all sides of area 1. Pin or glue fabric in place (**Fig. 3**).

Fig. 3

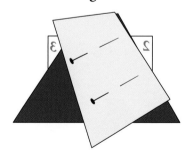

4. Rough cut a piece of tan fabric at least ½" larger on all sides than area 2. Turning foundation and fabric #1 over so that traced side of foundation is facing down, place fabric #2 on fabric #1, matching right sides. Pin fabric pieces in place (**Fig. 4**).

Fig. 4

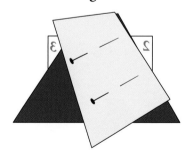

5. Turn foundation and fabric pieces over so that traced side of foundation is facing up; sew along line between areas 1 and 2, sewing a few stitches beyond beginning and end of line (**Fig. 5**).

Fig. 5

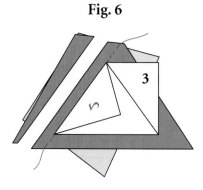

6. Fold back area 2 of foundation at stitching line and using ruler and rotary cutter, trim fabric pieces $^1/_4$" from seam (**Fig. 6**).

Fig. 6

7. Unfold foundation, and turn foundation and fabric pieces over so that traced side of foundation is facing down. Open out piece #2; press (**Fig. 7**).

Fig. 7

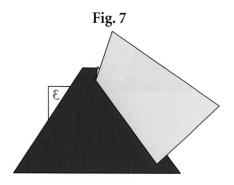

8. Continue in the same manner to cover area 3 with a piece of tan fabric. Using ruler and rotary cutter, trim fabric $^1/_4$" from outer edges of foundation as indicated by red line in **Fig. 8**. Carefully tear away foundation paper to make **Unit 4**. Make 6 **Unit 4's**.

Fig. 8

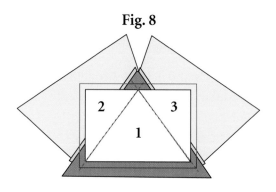

Unit 4 (make 6)

9. Sew 2 **large rectangles** and 1 **small rectangle** together to make **Unit 5**. Make 6 **Unit 5's**.

Unit 5 (make 6)

10. Sew 1 **Unit 4** and 1 **Unit 5** together to make **Tree Unit**. Make 6 **Tree Units**. *(Set aside 3 **Tree Units** for **Block D**).*

Tree Unit (make 6)

11. Sew 2 white **squares** and 1 red **square** together to make **Unit 6**.

Unit 6

12. Sew 3 **Tree Units** (1 of each green) and **Unit 6** together to make **Block B**.

Block B

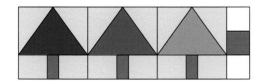

BLOCK C

Size (including seam allowance): $10^{1}/_{2}$" x $9^{1}/_{2}$"

1. Draw diagonal lines from corner to corner in both directions on wrong side of cream **large square**. With right sides together, place cream **large square** on top of red and yellow print **large square**. Stitch seam $^{1}/_{4}$" from each side of 1 drawn line (**Fig. 9**).

Fig. 9

2. Cut along drawn line between stitching and press open to make 2 **Large Triangle-Squares**.

Large Triangle-Squares (make 2)

3. On wrong side of 1 **Large Triangle-Square**, extend drawn line from corner of cream triangle to corner of red and yellow triangle.

79

4. Match 2 **Large Triangle-Squares** with contrasting fabrics facing and marked unit on top. Stitch seam $^1/_4$" on each side of drawn line (**Fig. 10**). Cut apart along drawn line to make 2 **Large Hourglass Units**; press **Large Hourglass Units** open.

Fig. 10

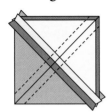

Large Hourglass Units (make 2)

5. Sew 2 **Large Hourglass Units** and 1 **large rectangle** together to make **Unit 7**.

Unit 7

6. Matching dots, sew 1 **A** and 1 **B** together to make **Unit 8**. Make 4 **Unit 8's**.

Unit 8 (make 4)

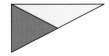

7. Sew 2 **Unit 8's** together to make **Unit 9**. Make 2 **Unit 9's**.

Unit 9 (make 2)

8. Sew 1 **Unit 9** and 2 **small rectangles** together to make **Unit 10**. Make 2 **Unit 10's**.

Unit 10 (make 2)

9. Sew **Unit 7** and 2 **Unit 10's** together to make **Unit 11**.

Unit 11

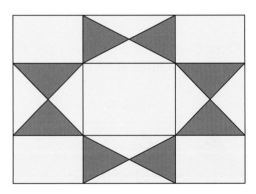

10. Sew 2 **small squares** and 1 **long rectangle** together to make **Unit 12**. Make 2 **Unit 12's**.

Unit 12 (make 2)

11. Sew **Unit 11** and 2 **Unit 12's** together to make **Unit 13**.

Unit 13

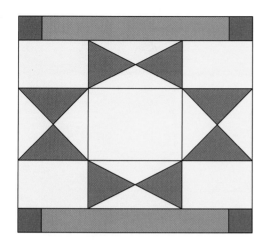

12. Arrange angel (**wings**, **head**, **hand**, **foot**, and **dress**) and **heart** in center of **Unit 13**; appliqué in place. Machine Satin Stitch wing and arm details. Using 2 strands of black floss, make French Knot for eye. Referring to photo, Couch Stitch 6 strands of rust floss with 1 strand of rust floss around top and back of head, making loops as desired to make hair for angel. (Couch Stitch is shown on page 110.)

Block C

BLOCK D
Size (including seam allowance): 16½" x 3½"

1. Sew 2 white **squares** and 1 red **square** together to make **Unit 14**.

Unit 14

2. Sew 2 **Star Units** (made in **Section 9**), 3 **Tree Units** (made in **Block B** of this **Section**), and **Unit 14** together to make **Block D**.

Block D

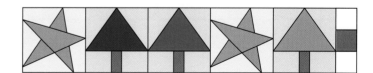

BLOCK E
Size (including seam allowance): 15¹/₂" x 3¹/₂"

1. Sew 2 red **strips** and 1 white **strip** together to make **Strip Set A**. Cut across **Strip Set A** at 1¹/₂" intervals to make 8 **Unit 15's**.

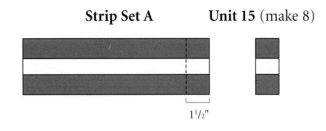

Strip Set A   **Unit 15** (make 8)

1¹/₂"

2. Sew 2 white **strips** and 1 red **strip** together to make **Strip Set B**. Cut across **Strip Set B** at 1¹/₂" intervals to make 7 **Unit 16's**.

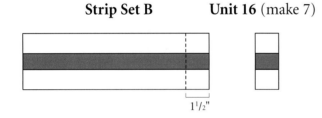

Strip Set B   **Unit 16** (make 7)

1¹/₂"

3. Sew 8 **Unit 15's** and 7 **Unit 16's** together to make **Block E**.

Block E

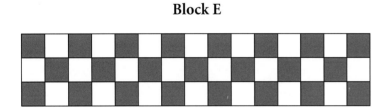

SECTION 14

1. Sew **Block B** and **Block C** together. Add **Block A** to make **Unit 17**.

Unit 17

2. Sew **Unit 17** and **Block D** together. Add **Block E** to complete **Section 14**.

Section 14

82

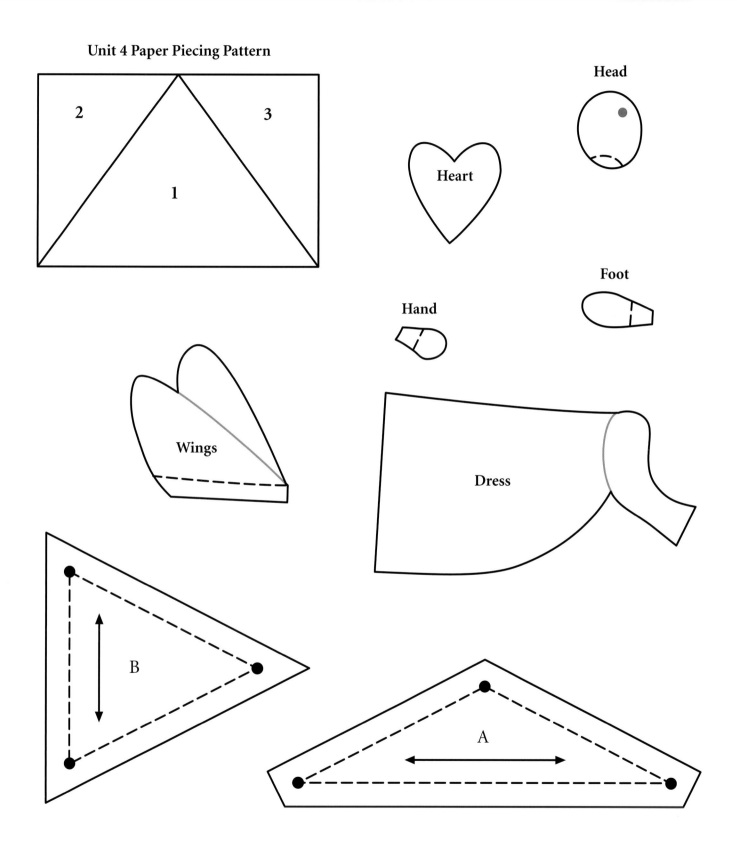

Unit 4 Paper Piecing Pattern

2

3

1

Head

Heart

Foot

Hand

Wings

Dress

B

A

83

BASKET WALL HANGING

Finished Wall Hanging Size: 46" x 46" (117 cm x 117 cm)
Finished Block Size: 6" x 6" (15 cm x 15 cm)

YARDAGE REQUIREMENTS

Yardage is based on 43"/44" (109 cm/112 cm) wide fabric.
  2⅝ yds (2.4 m) of black solid fabric
  ¼ yd (23 cm) *each* of 4 bright green print fabrics
  ¼ yd (23 cm) *each* of 4 bright blue print fabrics
  ¼ yd (23 cm) *each* of 4 bright purple print fabrics
  ¼ yd (23 cm) *each* of 4 bright pink print fabrics
  ⅛ yd (11 cm) of bright yellow print fabric
  3½ yds (3.2 m) of fabric for backing and hanging
    sleeve
You will also need:
  Approximately 5 yds (4.6 m) of ¼" (6 mm) wide
    green fusible bias tape
  Paper-backed fusible web
  54" x 54" (137 cm x 137 cm) square of batting

CUTTING OUT THE PIECES

*Refer to **Preparing Fusible Appliqué Pieces**, page 101, to cut out appliqué pieces. Appliquéd borders are cut larger than exact size to allow for raveling during appliquéing and will be trimmed before adding to quilt top. All other measurements include a ¼" seam allowance.*

From black solid fabric:

- Cut 2 strips 6½"w. From these strips, cut 9 **setting squares** 6½" x 6½".
- Cut 1 strip 9¾"w. From this strip, cut 3 squares 9¾" x 9¾". Cut squares *twice* diagonally to make 12 **setting triangles**.
- Cut 2 strips 2½"w. From these strips, cut 32 **squares** 2½" x 2½".
- Cut 2 strips 4⅞"w. From these strips, cut 16 squares 4⅞" x 4⅞". Cut squares *once* diagonally to make 32 **large triangles**.

- Cut 2 *lengthwise* **top/bottom outer borders** 7" x 47½".
- Cut 2 *lengthwise* **side outer borders** 7" x 38½".
- Cut 2 squares 5⅛" x 5⅛". Cut squares *once* diagonally to make 4 **corner setting triangles**.

From *each* bright green print fabric:

- Cut 1 **center square** 2½" x 2½" (for a total of 4 **center squares**).
- Cut 2 squares 2⅞" x 2⅞". Cut square *once* diagonally to make 4 **small triangles** (for a total of 16 **small triangles**).
- Cut 1 **basket handle** from pattern on page 32 (for a total of 4 **basket handles**).
- Cut 19 **small leaves** from pattern on page 41 (for a total of 76 **small leaves**).

Reserve remaining bright green print fabrics for pieced border and binding.

From *each* bright blue print, bright purple print, and bright pink print fabric:

- Cut 1 **center square** 2½" x 2½" (for a total of 12 **center squares**).
- Cut 2 squares 2⅞" x 2⅞". Cut square *once* diagonally to make 4 **small triangles** (for a total of 48 **small triangles**).
- Cut 1 **basket handle** from pattern on page 32 (for a total of 12 **basket handles**).
- Cut 3 **small flowers** from pattern on page 41 (for a total of 36 **small flowers**).

Reserve remaining bright blue print, bright purple print, and bright pink print fabrics for pieced border and binding.

From bright yellow print fabric:

- Cut 36 **small flower centers** from pattern on page 41.

MAKING THE BASKET WALL HANGING

*Follow **Piecing**, page 99, **Pressing**, page 100, and **Appliqué**, page 101, to make **Basket Wall Hanging**.*
Note: *For each **Block**, use 1 **basket handle** and 4 **small triangles** of the same print and 1 **center square** of another print of the same color.*

1. Matching raw edges of bottom of handle and long side of triangle, appliqué **basket handle** to 1 **large triangle** to make **Unit 1**.

Unit 1

2. Sew 1 **small triangle** and 1 black **square** together to make **Unit 2a**. Sew 1 **small triangle** and 1 black **square** together to make **Unit 2b**.

Unit 2a   Unit 2b

3. Sew 2 **small triangles** and 1 **center square** together to make **Unit 3**.

Unit 3

4. Sew **Unit 3** and 1 **large triangle** together to make **Unit 4**.

Unit 4

5. Sew **Unit 4**, **Unit 2a**, and **Unit 2b** together to make **Unit 5**

Unit 5

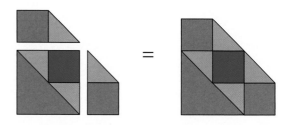

6. Sew **Unit 1** and **Unit 5** together to make **Block**.

Block

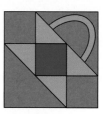

7. Repeat Steps 1 – 6 to make a total of 16 **Blocks**.

8. Referring to **Wall Hanging Center Assembly** diagram, sew **Blocks**, **setting squares**, **setting triangles,** and **corner setting triangles** together to make center section of wall hanging top.

9. Using assorted green, blue, purple, and pink prints, cut rectangles $1^1/2$" x various lengths. Sew together to make 2 **side inner borders** $1^1/2$" x $34^1/2$" and 2 **top/bottom inner borders** $1^1/2$" x $36^1/2$".

Wall Hanging Center Assembly

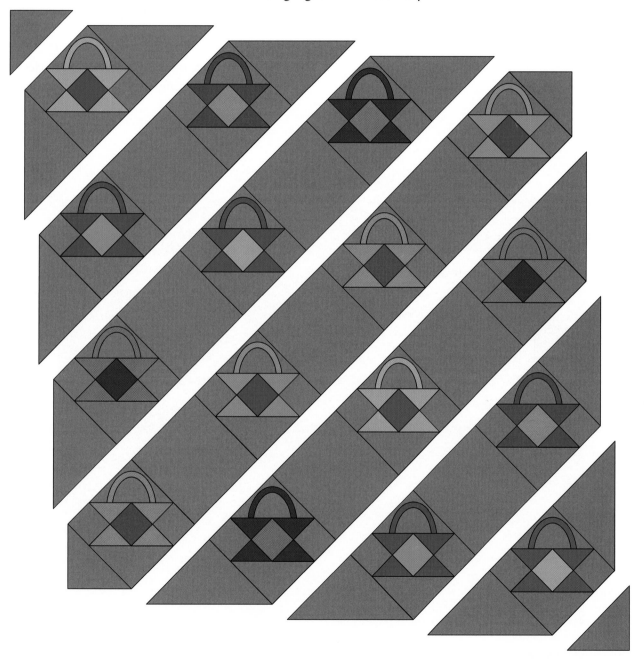

10. Add **side, top**, then **bottom inner borders** to wall hanging top.

11. Making sure appliqué design will fit into a 4" x 35" area, evenly space 8 **flowers** with **flower centers** across 1 **side outer border**; fuse into place. Fuse green bias tape around **flowers** for **vine**. Top Stitch **vine** $^1/_{16}$" from side edges. (***Note:*** *We used a #4 mm double needle to attach our vines.*) Arrange 17 **leaves** along **vine**; fuse into place. Appliqué **flowers, flower centers**, and **leaves**.

12. Making sure appliqué design is centered, trim **side outer border** to 5" x 36$^1/_2$". Repeat to make other **side outer border**.

13. Making sure appliqué design will fit into a 4" x 44" area, evenly space 10 **flowers** with **flower centers** across **top outer border**; fuse into place. Fuse green bias tape around **flowers** for **vine**. Top Stitch **vine** $^1/_{16}$" from side edges. Arrange 21 **leaves** along vine; fuse into place. Appliqué **flowers, flower centers**, and **leaves**.

14. Making sure appliqué design is centered, trim **top outer border** to 5" x 45$^1/_2$". Repeat to make **bottom outer border**.

15. Add **side, top**, then **bottom outer borders** to complete wall hanging top.

Wall Hanging Diagram

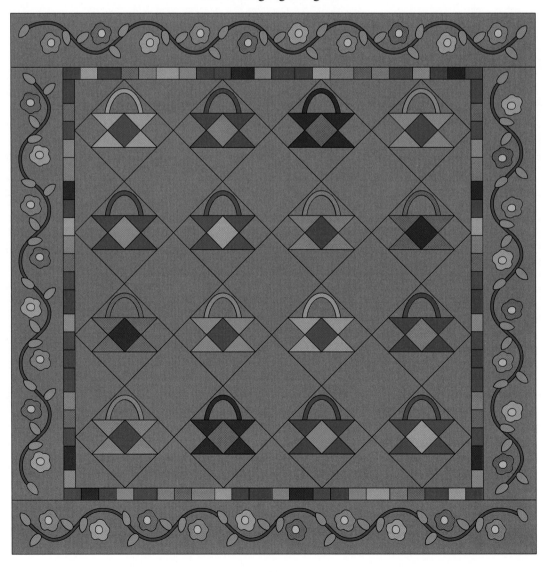

COMPLETING THE WALL HANGING

1. Follow **Quilting**, page 102, to mark, layer, and quilt. Our wall hanging is machine quilted in the ditch with a flower motif quilted in each setting square (see photo, below). Bright variegated thread was used for quilting.

2. Follow **Making a Hanging Sleeve**, page 106, to add a hanging sleeve to back of wall hanging.

3. To make spiral bias binding, cut $2^1/_2$"w bias pieces of various lengths from remaining green, blue, purple, and pink left over fabric scraps. Sew pieces together, pressing seam allowances to 1 side, to form $5^3/_8$ yds of $2^1/_2$" w bias binding. Follow **Binding**, page 106, to bind wall hanging with mitered corners.

CHILDREN WALL HANGING

Finished Size: 17" x 17" (43 cm x 43 cm)

YARDAGE REQUIREMENTS

Yardage is based on 43"/44" (109 cm/112 cm) wide fabric.

STAR ROW

9" x 22" (23 cm x 56 cm) piece of cream print fabric #1

12" x 6" (30 cm x 15 cm) piece *each* of 3 gold print fabrics

CHILD ROW

9" x 22" (23 cm x 56 cm) piece of cream solid fabric

6" x 6" (15 cm x 15 cm) piece of light pink solid fabric

10" x 8" (25 cm x 20 cm) piece of green print fabric

6" x 4" (15 cm x 10 cm) piece of red print fabric

5" x 3" (13 cm x 8 cm) piece of dark blue solid fabric

WHEAT ROW

13" x 13" (33 cm x 33 cm) piece of cream print fabric #2

4" x 4" (10 cm x 10 cm) piece *each* of 4 gold print fabrics

SASHING, BORDERS, BACKING, AND BINDING

$^1/_2$ yd (46 cm) *total* of assorted gold, blue, red, and green print fabrics

$^7/_8$ yd (80 cm) of fabric for backing and hanging sleeve

$^1/_2$ yd (46 cm) of fabric for binding

You will also need:

21" x 21" (53 cm x 53 cm) square of batting

Black and brown embroidery floss

Gold and dark brown size #3 pearl cotton

Paper-backed fusible web

Stabilizer

Lightweight copy paper or typing paper

CUTTING OUT THE PIECES

*Refer to **Preparing Fusible Appliqué Pieces**, page 101, to cut appliqué pieces. Measurements include a $^1/_4$" seam allowance.*

CHILD ROW

From cream solid fabric:

- Cut 4 **rectangle A's** $3^1/_2$" x $1^3/_4$".
- Cut 4 **square D's** $1^1/_2$" x $1^1/_2$".
- Cut 2 **rectangle F's** $^3/_4$" x $1^1/_2$".
- Cut 4 **rectangle G's** $1^1/_2$" x $1^1/_4$".
- Cut 4 **rectangle H's** $1^1/_2$" x 2".
- Cut 2 **rectangle J's** $^3/_4$" x 2".

Reserve remaining cream solid fabric for paper piecing.

From light pink solid fabric:

- Cut 8 **square C's** 1" x 1".
- Cut 4 **rectangle E's** $^7/_8$" x $1^1/_2$".
- Cut 4 **heads** from pattern on page 64.

From green print fabric:

- Cut 2 **rectangle B's** $2^1/_2$" x 1".

Reserve remaining green print fabric for paper piecing.

From red print fabric:

- Cut 2 **rectangle B's** $2^1/_2$" x 1".
- Cut 2 **rectangle G's** $1^1/_2$" x $1^1/_4$".

From dark blue solid fabric:

- Cut 4 **rectangle I's** $^7/_8$" x 2".

WHEAT ROW

From cream print fabric #2:

- Cut 4 **background squares** $5^1/_2$" x $5^1/_2$".

From *each* 4" x 4" piece of gold print fabric:

- Cut 1 **wheat sheaf** from pattern on page 69 for a total of 4 **sheaves**.

SASHING AND BINDING

From assorted gold, blue, red, and green print fabrics:

- Cut 24 **small squares** $1^1/_2$" x $1^1/_2$".

Reserve remaining assorted print fabrics for borders.

From fabric for binding:

- Cut 1 **square for binding** 15" x 15".

91

MAKING THE CHILDREN WALL HANGING

*Follow **Piecing**, page 99, **Pressing**, page 100, and **Appliqué**, page 101, to make **Children Wall Hanging**.*

1. Using cream print #1 and the 12" x 6" pieces of gold print, follow Steps 1 – 11 of **Block A**, **Section 9**, pages 47 - 48, to make 4 **Star Units**. Sew 4 **Star Units** together to complete **Star Row**.

Star Row

2. Substituting green print for light blue print, red print for red polka dot, and dark blue solid for dark blue print, and using dark brown and gold pearl cotton for hair, follow Steps 1 – 17 of **Block A**, **Section 11**, pages 59 - 61, to complete **Child Row**. (See photos, page 93.)

Child Row

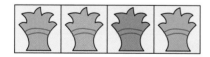

3. Using cream print #2 and 4" x 4" pieces of gold prints, follow Steps 1 – 3 of **Block A**, **Section 12**, page 67, to make **Wheat Row**.

Wheat Row

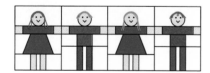

4. Arranging colors in random order, sew 12 **sashing squares** together to make **Sashing Row**. Make 2 **Sashing Rows**.

Sashing Row (make 2)

5. Sew **Rows** and **Sashing Rows** together to complete center section of wall hanging.

Center Section of Wall Hanging

6. Cut $2^{1}/_{2}$" rectangles of various widths from remaining assorted prints. Sew enough rectangles together to make 2 **side borders** $2^{1}/_{2}$" x $12^{1}/_{2}$". Sew enough rectangles together to make 2 **top/bottom borders** $2^{1}/_{2}$" x $16^{1}/_{2}$".

7. Add **side**, **top**, then **bottom borders** to complete wall hanging top.

92

COMPLETING THE WALL HANGING

1. Follow **Quilting**, page 102, to mark, layer, and quilt. Our wall hanging is machine quilted in the ditch.
2. Using **square for binding**, follow **Binding**, page 106, to bind wall hanging using $2^1/2$"w bias binding with mitered corners.

Wall Hanging Diagram

WOOL FELT TOTE

Approximate Size: 10$\frac{1}{2}$" x 12" (27 cm x 30 cm) plus handles

YARDAGE REQUIREMENTS

Yardage for wool felt is based on 38" (97 cm) wide fabric. Yardage for cotton fabric is based on 43"/44" (109 cm/112 cm) wide fabric.

- $\frac{1}{8}$ yd (11 cm) of red and white striped cotton fabric
- $\frac{1}{2}$ yd (46 cm) of grey wool felt
- $\frac{1}{2}$ yd (46 cm) of red wool felt
- Scraps of black, white, blue, and green wool felt

You will also need:

- 1 yd (91 cm) of $\frac{1}{4}$" (6.35 mm) diameter cord
- 1$\frac{1}{2}$ yds (1.4 m) of $\frac{3}{8}$" (9.5 mm) wide red grosgrain ribbon
- Fabric glue stick
- Black, white, red, blue, green, and grey embroidery floss
- Pinking shears or rotary cutter with pinking blade

CUTTING OUT THE PIECES

Before cutting, wash each color felt separately in hot water, rinse in cold water, and tumble dry on warm setting to create the "fuzzy" look of the tote. Felt will shrink considerably. Trace appliqué patterns onto paper; pin to felt and cut along drawn lines.

From red and white striped fabric:

- Cut 1 **long strip** 2" x 30".
- Cut 1 **short strip** 2" x 23".

From grey wool felt:

- Cut 1 **large rectangle** 12" x 24".

From red wool felt:

- Cut 1 **top band** 2" x 23".
- Cut 4 **handle strips** 1$\frac{1}{2}$" x 20".
- Cut 1 **small heart** from pattern on page 45.
- Cut 4 rectangles 1$\frac{1}{4}$" x $\frac{3}{8}$" for **flag short stripes** for appliqué.
- Cut 4 rectangles 2" x $\frac{3}{8}$" for **flag long stripes** for appliqué.

From white wool felt:

- Cut 4 rectangles 2" x 1$\frac{1}{2}$" for **flag backgrounds** for appliqué.

From blue wool felt:

- Cut 4 squares $\frac{3}{4}$" x $\frac{3}{4}$" for **flag star fields** for appliqué.

From black wool felt:

- Cut 4 **flagpoles** $\frac{1}{4}$" x 4$\frac{1}{2}$" for appliqué.

From green wool felt:

- Cut 8 **large leaves** from pattern on page 45.
- Cut 8 **small leaves** from pattern on page 45.

MAKING THE WOOL FELT TOTE

*Follow **Piecing**, page 99, **Pressing**, page 100, to make tote. Use ¹/₂" seam allowances throughout. Appliqués are attached using 2 strands of matching floss and small **Straight Stitches**. Use small dots of glue to hold appliqué pieces in place before stitching.*

1. Glue 1 **flag star field**, 1 **flag short stripe**, and 1 **flag long stripe** on each **flag background**. Appliqué **stripes** and **fields** to **backgrounds** to make 4 **flags**.

Flag (make 4)

2. Matching wrong sides and short raw edges, fold **large rectangle** in half. Center and arrange **flags**, **flagpoles**, **leaves**, and **heart** on 1 side of folded **rectangle**; glue in place (**Fig. 1**). Unfold rectangle and appliqué design in place.

Fig. 1

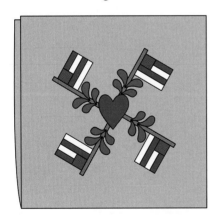

3. To make cording, lay cord along center of **long strip** on wrong side of fabric; fold strip over cord. Using a zipper foot, machine baste close to cord. Cut 2 cording strips 12" long; trim seam allowances to ¹/₂".

4. Matching raw edges, baste cording to front of large rectangle at sides (**Fig. 2**). Matching right sides and short raw edges, fold **large rectangle** in half. Sew sides of tote close to cording. Do *not* turn right side out.

Fig. 2

96

5. To form bottom corners of tote, match side seams to fold (bottom of tote) and sew across each corner $1^1/_4$" from end of side seam (**Fig. 3**). Turn tote right side out.

Fig. 3

$1^1/_4$"

6. Matching right sides and raw edges, sew short ends of **short strip** together to form loop; press seam allowances open. Fold loop lengthwise with wrong sides together and raw edges matching; press. Matching raw edges of loop to top edge of tote, baste loop to right side of tote $1/_2$" from raw edges.

7. Matching right sides and raw edges, sew short ends of **top band** together to form loop; press seam allowances open. Using pinking shears or rotary cutter with pinking blade, trim $1/_4$" from 1 raw edge of loop. With wrong sides together and matching raw edge and pinked edge, press loop in half.

8. Place folded **top band** over top edge of tote. Fold pinked edge of **top band** up and stitch **top band** to tote $1/_2$" from top edge of tote (**Fig. 4**)

Fig. 4

9. To make each handle, layer 2 **handle strips**. Using 4 strands of grey floss and a Running Stitch, make 2 parallel lines of stitches $1/_2$" apart along the length of the **handle strips**. Cut two 27" lengths of ribbon. Thread ribbon between stitched rows of each handle using safety pin (**Fig. 5**). Cutting through both layers of felt with pinking shears or rotary cutter with pinking blade, trim edges of **handle strips** $1/_4$" from stitching. Trim ends of ribbon even with **handle strips**. Repeat with remaining **handle strips**.

Fig. 5

10. Turn tote wrong side out. With **top band** still unfolded, machine stitch handles to tote (**Fig. 6**) $1^3/_4$" from side seams of tote.

Fig. 6

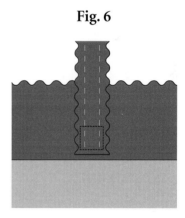

11. Turn tote right side out. Referring to photo, page 95, fold pinked edge of **top band** to right side of tote. Using 4 strands of grey floss and Running Stitch, stitch through all layers $1/_4$" from pinked edge of **top band**. Make large Cross Stitches on **top band** at ends of handles.

GENERAL INSTRUCTIONS

To make your quilting easier and more enjoyable, we encourage you to carefully read all of the general instructions, study the color photographs, and familiarize yourself with the individual project instructions before beginning a project.

FABRICS

SELECTING FABRICS

Choose high-quality, medium-weight 100% cotton fabrics. All-cotton fabrics hold a crease better, fray less, and are easier to quilt than cotton/polyester blends.

Yardage requirements listed for each project are based on 43"/44" wide fabric with a "usable" width of 40" after shrinkage and trimming selvages. Actual usable width will probably vary slightly from fabric to fabric. Our recommended yardage lengths should be adequate for occasional re-squaring of fabric when many cuts are required.

PREPARING FABRICS

We recommend that all fabrics be washed, dried, and pressed before cutting. If fabrics are not pre-washed, washing the finished quilt will cause shrinkage and give it a more "antiqued" look and feel. Bright and dark colors, which may run, should always be washed before cutting. After washing and drying fabric, fold lengthwise with wrong sides together and matching selvages.

ROTARY CUTTING

Rotary cutting has brought speed and accuracy to quiltmaking by allowing quilters to easily cut strips of fabric and then cut those strips into smaller pieces.

- Place fabric on work surface with fold closest to you.

- Cut all strips from the selvage-to-selvage width of the fabric unless otherwise indicated in project instructions.

- Square left edge of fabric using rotary cutter and rulers (**Figs. 1 - 2**).

Fig. 1

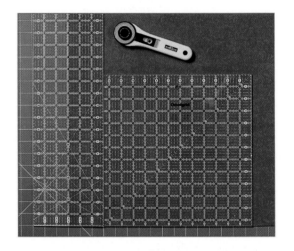

Fig. 2

- To cut each strip required for a project, place ruler over cut edge of fabric, aligning desired marking on ruler with cut edge; make cut (**Fig. 3**).

Fig. 3

- When cutting several strips from a single piece of fabric, it is important to make sure that cuts remain at a perfect right angle to the fold; re-square fabric as needed.

TEMPLATE CUTTING

Our piecing template patterns have 2 lines – a solid cutting line and a dashed line showing the $^1/4$" seam allowance. (Patterns for appliqué pieces do not include seam allowances.)

1. To make a template from a pattern, use a permanent fine-point pen and a ruler to carefully trace pattern onto template plastic, making sure to transfer any alignment markings. Cut out template along inner edge of drawn line. Check template against original pattern for accuracy.
2. Place template face down on wrong side of fabric (unless otherwise indicated in project instructions), aligning grain line on template with straight grain of fabric. Use a sharp fabric-marking pencil to draw around template. Transfer all alignment markings to fabric. Cut out fabric piece using scissors or rotary cutting equipment.

PIECING

Precise cutting, followed by accurate piecing, will ensure that all pieces of quilt top fit together well.

HAND PIECING

- Use ruler and sharp fabric marking pencil to draw all seam lines and transfer any alignment markings onto back of cut pieces.

- Matching right sides, pin 2 pieces together, using pins to mark corners.

- Use Running Stitch to sew pieces together along drawn line, backstitching at beginning and end of seam.

- Do not extend stitches into seam allowances.

- Run 5 or 6 stitches onto needle before pulling needle through fabric.

- To add stability, backstitch every $^3/4$" to 1".

MACHINE PIECING

- Set sewing machine stitch length for approximately 11 stitches per inch.

- Use neutral-colored general-purpose sewing thread (not quilting thread) in needle and in bobbin.

- An accurate $^1/4$" seam allowance is *essential*. Presser feet that are $^1/4$" wide are available for most sewing machines.

- When piecing, always place pieces right sides together and match raw edges; pin if necessary.

- Chain piecing saves time and will usually result in more accurate piecing.

- Trim away points of seam allowances that extend beyond edges of sewn pieces.

SEWING STRIP SETS

When there are several strips to assemble into a strip set, first sew strips together into pairs, then sew pairs together to form strip set. To help avoid distortion, sew seams in opposite directions (**Fig. 4**).

Fig. 4

SEWING ACROSS SEAM INTERSECTIONS

When sewing across intersection of 2 seams, place pieces right sides together and match seams exactly, making sure seam allowances are pressed in opposite directions (**Fig. 5**).

Fig. 5

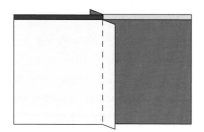

SEWING SHARP POINTS

To ensure sharp points when joining triangular or diagonal pieces, stitch across the center of the "X" (shown in pink) formed on wrong side by previous seams (**Fig. 6**).

Fig. 6

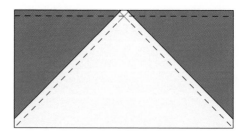

PRESSING

• Use steam iron set on "Cotton" for all pressing (with the exception of "Wool" setting for wool felt used in Wool Felt Tote).

• Press after sewing each seam.

• Seam allowances are almost always pressed to 1 side, usually toward darker fabric. However, to reduce bulk it may occasionally be necessary to press seam allowances toward the lighter fabric or even to press them open.

• To prevent dark fabric seam allowance from showing through light fabric, trim darker seam allowance slightly narrower than lighter seam allowance.

• To press long seams, such as those in long strip sets, without curving or other distortion, lay strips across width of the ironing board.

APPLIQUÉ

PREPARING FUSIBLE APPLIQUÉ PIECES

White or light-colored fabrics may need to be lined with fusible interfacing before applying fusible web to prevent darker fabrics from showing through.

1. Place paper-backed fusible web, paper side up, over appliqué pattern. Trace pattern, including detail lines, onto paper side of web with pencil as many times as indicated in project instructions for a single fabric. ***Note:*** Some pieces may be given as measurements, such as a 2" x 4" rectangle, instead of drawn patterns. Use ruler to draw shapes onto paper side of web.
2. Follow manufacturer's instructions to fuse traced patterns to wrong side of fabrics. Do not remove paper backing.
3. Use scissors to cut out appliqué pieces along traced lines; use rotary cutting equipment to cut out appliqué pieces given as measurements.
4. Before removing paper backing, lightly mark all detail lines on fabric side of appliqué pieces with pencil. Most of the details are simple and may be marked free-hand. For more accuracy, hold pieces against sunny window pane and trace details onto fabric.

SATIN STITCH APPLIQUÉ

A good satin stitch is a thick, smooth, almost solid line of zigzag stitching that covers the exposed raw edges of appliqué pieces.

1. Pin stabilizer, such as paper or any of the commercially available products, on wrong side of background fabric before stitching appliqués in place.
2. Thread sewing machine with general-purpose thread; use general-purpose thread that matches background fabric in bobbin.
3. Set sewing machine for a medium (approximately ¹/₈") zigzag stitch and a short stitch length. Slightly loosening the top tension may yield a smoother stitch.

4. Begin by stitching 2 or 3 stitches in place (drop feed dogs or set stitch length at 0) to anchor thread. Most of the Satin Stitch should be on the appliqué with the right edge of the stitch falling at the outside edge of the appliqué. Stitch over all exposed raw edges of appliqué pieces.
5. (***Note:*** Dots on **Figs. 7 – 12** indicate where to leave needle in fabric when pivoting.) For outside corners, stitch just past corner, stopping with needle in background fabric (**Fig. 7**). Raise presser foot. Pivot project, lower presser foot, and stitch adjacent side (**Fig. 8**).

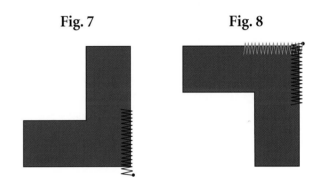

Fig. 7   **Fig. 8**

6. For inside corners, stitch just past corner, stopping with needle in appliqué fabric (**Fig. 9**). Raise presser foot. Pivot project, lower presser foot, and stitch adjacent side (**Fig. 10**).

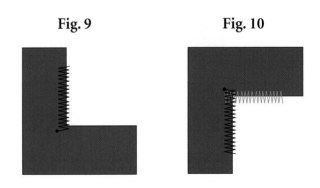

Fig. 9   **Fig. 10**

7. When stitching outside curves, stop with needle in background fabric. Raise presser foot and pivot project as needed. Lower presser foot and continue stitching, pivoting as often as necessary to follow curve (**Fig. 11**).

Fig. 11

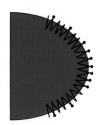

8. When stitching inside curves, stop with needle in appliqué fabric. Raise presser foot and pivot project as needed. Lower presser foot and continue stitching, pivoting as often as necessary to follow curve (**Fig. 12**).

Fig. 12

9. Do not backstitch at end of stitching. Pull threads to wrong side of background fabric; knot thread and trim ends.
10. Carefully tear away stabilizer.

QUILTING
*Quilting holds the 3 layers (top, batting, and backing) of the quilt together and can be done by hand or machine. Because marking, layering, and quilting are interrelated and may be done in different orders depending on circumstances, please read entire **Quilting** section before beginning project.*

TYPES OF QUILTING DESIGNS
"IN THE DITCH" QUILTING
Quilting along seamlines or along edges of appliquéd pieces is called "in the ditch" quilting. This type of quilting should be done on side opposite seam allowance and does not have to be marked.

OUTLINE QUILTING
Quilting a consistent distance, usually $1/4$", from seam or appliqué is called "outline" quilting. Outline quilting may be marked, or $1/4$" masking tape may be placed along seamlines for quilting guide. (Do not leave tape on quilt longer than necessary, since it may leave an adhesive residue.)

MOTIF QUILTING
Quilting a design, such as a feathered wreath, is called "motif" quilting. This type of quilting should be marked before basting quilt layers together.

ECHO QUILTING
Quilting that follows the outline of an appliquéd or pieced design with 2 or more parallel lines is called "echo" quilting. This type of quilting does not need to be marked.

CHANNEL QUILTING
Quilting with straight, parallel lines is called "channel" quilting. This type of quilting may be marked or stitched using a guide.

CROSSHATCH QUILTING

Quilting straight lines in a grid pattern is called "crosshatch" quilting. Lines may be stitched parallel to edges of quilt or stitched diagonally. This type of quilting may be marked or stitched using a guide.

MEANDERING QUILTING

Quilting in random curved lines and swirls is called "meandering" quilting. Quilting lines should not cross or touch each other. This type of quilting does not need to be marked.

STIPPLE QUILTING

Meandering quilting that is very closely spaced is called "stipple" quilting. Stippling will flatten the area quilted and is often stitched in background areas to raise appliquéd or pieced designs. This type of quilting does not need to be marked.

MARKING QUILTING LINES

Quilting lines may be marked using fabric marking pencils, chalk markers, water or air soluble pens, or lead pencils.

Simple quilting designs may be marked with chalk or chalk pencil after basting. A small area may be marked, then quilted, before moving to next area to be marked. Intricate designs should be marked before basting using a more durable marker.

Caution: Some marks may be permanently set by pressing. **Test** different markers **on scrap fabric** to find one that marks clearly and can be thoroughly removed.

A wide variety of pre-cut quilting stencils, as well as entire books of quilting patterns, are available. Using a stencil makes it easier to mark intricate or repetitive designs.

To make a stencil from a pattern, center template plastic over pattern and use a permanent marker to trace pattern onto plastic. Use a craft knife with single or double blade to cut channels along traced lines (**Fig. 13**).

Fig. 13

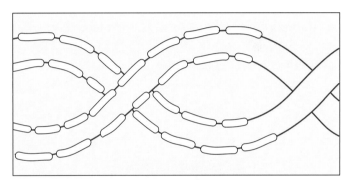

PREPARING THE BACKING

To allow for slight shifting of quilt top during quilting, backing should be approximately 4" larger on all sides. Yardage requirements listed for quilt backings are calculated for 43/44"w fabric. Using 90"w or 108"w fabric for the backing of a bed-sized quilt may eliminate piecing. To piece a backing using 43/44"w fabric (with a "usable" width of 40"), use the following instructions.

1. Measure length and width of quilt top; add 8" to each measurement.
2. Cut backing fabric into 2 lengths slightly longer than determined **length** measurement. Trim selvages. Place lengths with right sides facing and sew long edges together, forming tube (**Fig. 14**). Match seams and press along 1 fold (**Fig. 15**). Cut along pressed fold to form single piece (**Fig. 16**).

Fig. 14	**Fig. 15**	**Fig. 16**

3. Trim backing to size determined in Step 1; press seam allowances open.

CHOOSING THE BATTING

The appropriate batting will make quilting easier. For fine hand quilting, choose low-loft batting. All cotton or cotton/polyester blend battings work well for machine quilting because the cotton helps "grip" quilt layers. If quilt is to be tied, a high-loft batting, sometimes called extra-loft or fat batting, may be used to make quilt "fluffy."

Types of batting include cotton, polyester, cotton/polyester blend, wool, cotton/wool blend, and silk.

When selecting batting, refer to package labels for characteristics and care instructions. Cut batting same size as prepared backing.

ASSEMBLING THE QUILT

1. Examine wrong side of quilt top closely; trim any seam allowances and clip any threads that may show through front of the quilt. Press quilt top, being careful not to "set" any marked quilting lines.
2. Place backing **wrong** side up on flat surface. Use masking tape to tape edges of backing to surface. Place batting on top of backing fabric. Smooth batting gently, being careful not to stretch or tear. Center quilt top **right** side up on batting.
3. If hand quilting, begin in center and work toward outer edges to hand baste all layers together. Use long stitches and place basting lines approximately 4" apart (**Fig. 17**). Smooth fullness or wrinkles toward outer edges.

Fig. 17

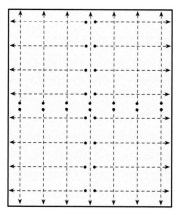

4. If machine quilting, use 1" rustproof safety pins to "pin-baste" all layers together, spacing pins approximately 4" apart. Begin at center and work toward outer edges to secure all layers. If possible, place pins away from areas that will be quilted, although pins may be removed as needed when quilting.

HAND QUILTING

The quilting stitch is a basic running stitch that forms a broken line on quilt top and backing. Stitches on quilt top and backing should be straight and equal in length.

1. Secure center of quilt in hoop or frame. Check quilt top and backing to make sure they are smooth. To help prevent puckers, always begin quilting in the center of quilt and work toward outside edges.

2. Thread needle with 18" - 20" length of quilting thread; knot 1 end. Using thimble, insert needle into quilt top and batting approximately $1/2$" from quilting line. Bring needle up on quilting line (**Fig. 18**); when knot catches on quilt top, give thread a quick, short pull to "pop" knot through fabric into batting (**Fig. 19**).

Fig. 18	**Fig. 19**

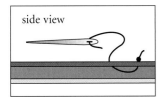 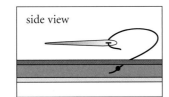

3. Holding needle with sewing hand and placing other hand underneath quilt, use thimble to push tip of needle down through all layers. As soon as needle touches finger underneath, use that finger to push tip of needle only back up through layers to top of quilt. (The amount of needle showing above fabric determines length of quilting stitch.) Referring to **Fig. 20**, rock needle up and down, taking 3 - 6 stitches before bringing needle and thread completely through layers. Check back of quilt to make sure stitches are going through all layers. If necessary, make 1 stitch at a time when quilting through seam allowances or along curves and corners.

Fig. 20

4. At end of thread, knot thread close to fabric and "pop" knot into batting; clip thread close to fabric.

5. Move hoop as often as necessary. Thread may be left dangling and picked up again after returning to that part of quilt.

MACHINE QUILTING METHODS

Use general-purpose thread in bobbin. Do not use quilting thread. Thread the needle of machine with general-purpose thread or transparent monofilament thread to make quilting blend with quilt top fabrics. Use decorative thread, such as a metallic or contrasting-color general-purpose thread, to make quilting lines stand out more.

STRAIGHT LINE QUILTING

The term "straight-line" is somewhat deceptive, since curves (especially gentle ones) as well as straight lines can be stitched with this technique.

1. Set stitch length for 6 - 10 stitches per inch and attach walking foot to sewing machine.

2. Determine which section of quilt will have longest continuous quilting line, oftentimes area from center top to center bottom. Roll up and secure each edge of quilt to help reduce the bulk, keeping fabrics smooth. Smaller projects may not need to be rolled.

3. Begin stitching on longest quilting line, using very short stitches for the first $1/4$" to "lock" quilting. Stitch across project, using 1 hand on each side of walking foot to slightly spread fabric and to guide fabric through machine. Lock stitches at end of quilting line.

4. Continue machine quilting, stitching longer quilting lines first to stabilize quilt before moving on to other areas.

FREE MOTION QUILTING

Free motion quilting may be free form or may follow a marked pattern.

1. Attach darning foot to sewing machine and lower or cover feed dogs.

2. Position quilt under darning foot. Lower presser foot. Holding top thread, take 1 stitch and pull bobbin thread to top of quilt. To "lock" beginning of quilting line, hold top and bobbin threads while making 3 to 5 stitches in place.

3. Use 1 hand on each side of darning foot to slightly spread fabric and to move fabric through the machine. Even stitch length is achieved by using smooth, flowing hand motion and steady machine speed. Slow machine speed and fast hand movement will create long stitches. Fast machine speed and slow hand movement will create short stitches. Move quilt sideways, back and forth, in a circular motion, or in a random motion to create desired designs; do not rotate quilt. Lock stitches at end of each quilting line.

MAKING A HANGING SLEEVE

Attaching a hanging sleeve to back of wall hanging or quilt before the binding is added allows project to be displayed on wall.

1. Measure width of quilt top edge and subtract 1". Cut piece of fabric 7"w by determined measurement.

2. Press short edges of fabric piece $1/4$" to wrong side; press edges $1/4$" to wrong side again and machine stitch in place.

3. Matching wrong sides, fold piece in half lengthwise to form tube.

4. Follow project instructions to sew binding to quilt top and to trim backing and batting. Before blindstitching binding to backing, match raw edges and stitch hanging sleeve to center top edge on back of quilt.

5. Finish binding quilt, treating hanging sleeve as part of backing.

6. Blindstitch bottom of hanging sleeve to backing, taking care not to stitch through to front of quilt.

BINDING

Binding encloses the raw edges of quilt. Because of its stretchiness, bias binding works well for binding projects with curves or rounded corners and tends to lie smooth and flat in any given circumstance. Binding may also be cut from straight lengthwise or crosswise grain of fabric.

MAKING CONTINUOUS BIAS STRIP BINDING

Bias strips for binding can simply be cut and pieced to desired length. However, when a long length of binding is needed, the "continuous" method is quick and accurate.

1. Cut square from binding fabric the size indicated in project instructions. Cut square in half diagonally to make 2 triangles.

2. With right sides together and using ¹/₄" seam allowance, sew triangles together (**Fig. 21**); press seam allowances open.

Fig. 21

3. On wrong side of fabric, draw lines the width of binding as specified in project instructions, usually 2¹/₂" (**Fig. 22**). Cut off any remaining fabric less than this width.

Fig. 22

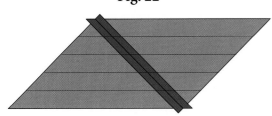

4. With right sides inside, bring short edges together to form tube; match raw edges so that first drawn line of top section meets second drawn line of bottom section (**Fig. 23**).

Fig. 23

5. Carefully pin edges together by inserting pins through drawn lines at point where drawn lines intersect, making sure pins go through intersections on both sides. Using ¹/₄" seam allowance, sew edges together; press seam allowances open.

6. To cut continuous strip, begin cutting along first drawn line (**Fig. 24**). Continue cutting along drawn line around tube.

Fig. 24

7. Trim ends of bias strip square.
8. Matching wrong sides and raw edges, press bias strip in half lengthwise to complete binding.

ATTACHING BINDING WITH MITERED CORNERS

1. Beginning with 1 end near center on bottom edge of quilt, lay binding around quilt to make sure that seams in binding will not end up at a corner. Adjust placement if necessary. Matching raw edges of binding to raw edge of quilt top, pin binding to right side of quilt along 1 edge.

2. When you reach first corner, mark ¼" from corner of quilt top (**Fig. 25**).

Fig. 25

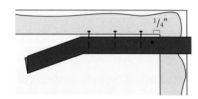

3. Beginning approximately 10" from end of binding and using ¼" seam allowance, sew binding to quilt, backstitching at beginning of stitching and at mark (**Fig. 26**). Lift needle out of fabric and clip thread.

Fig. 26

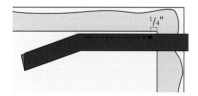

4. Fold binding as shown in **Figs. 27 - 28** and pin binding to adjacent side, matching raw edges. Upon reaching the next corner, mark ¼" from edge of quilt top.

Fig. 27   **Fig. 28**

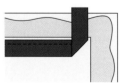   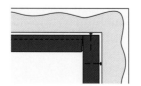

5. Backstitching at edge of quilt top, sew pinned binding to quilt (**Fig. 29**); backstitch at the next mark. Lift needle out of fabric and clip thread.

Fig. 29

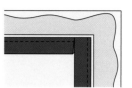

6. Continue sewing binding to quilt, stopping approximately 10" from starting point (**Fig. 30**).

Fig. 30

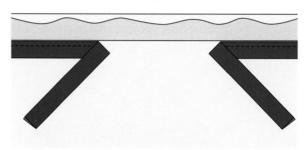

7. Bring beginning and end of binding to center of opening and fold each end back, leaving a ¼" space between folds (**Fig. 31**). Finger-press folds.

Fig. 31

8. Unfold ends of binding and draw a line across wrong side in finger-pressed crease. Draw a line through the lengthwise pressed fold of binding at same spot to create a cross mark. With edge of ruler at marked cross, line up 45° angle marking on ruler with one long side of binding. Draw a diagonal line from edge to edge. Repeat on remaining end, making sure that the two diagonal lines are angled the same way (**Fig. 32**).

Fig. 32

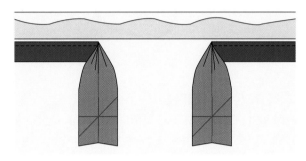

9. Matching right sides and diagonal lines, pin binding ends together at right angles (**Fig. 33**).

Fig. 33

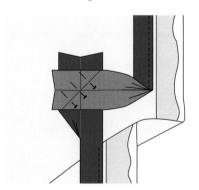

10. Machine stitch along diagonal line (**Fig. 34**), removing pins as you stitch.

Fig. 34

11. Lay binding against quilt to double check that it is correct length.
12. Trim binding ends, leaving $^1/_4$" seam allowance; press seam allowances open. Stitch binding to quilt.
13. If using $2^1/_2$"w binding (finished size $^1/_2$"), trim backing and batting a scant $^1/_4$" larger than quilt top so that batting and backing will fill the binding when it is folded over to quilt backing.
14. On 1 edge of quilt, fold binding over to quilt backing and pin pressed edge in place, covering stitching line (**Fig. 35**). On adjacent side, fold binding over, forming a mitered corner (**Fig. 36**). Repeat to pin remainder of binding in place.

Fig. 35   **Fig. 36**

15. Blindstitch binding to backing, taking care not to stitch through to front of quilt.

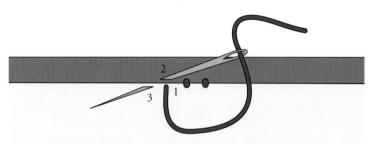

SIGNING AND DATING YOUR QUILT

A completed quilt is a work of art and should be signed and dated. There are many different ways to do this and numerous books on the subject. The label should reflect the style of the quilt, the occasion or person for which it was made, and the quilter's own particular talents. Following are suggestions for recording the history of the quilt or adding a sentiment for future generations.

- Embroider quilter's name, date, and any additional information on quilt top or backing. Matching floss, such as cream floss on white border, will leave a subtle record. Bright or contrasting floss will make the information stand out.

- Make label from muslin and use permanent marker to write information. Use different colored permanent markers to make label more decorative. Stitch label to back of quilt.

- Use photo-transfer paper to add image to white or cream fabric label. Stitch label to back of quilt.

- Piece an extra block from quilt top pattern to use as label. Add information with permanent fabric pen. Appliqué block to back of quilt.

- Write message on appliquéd design from quilt top. Attach appliqué to back of the quilt.

HAND STITCHES
BLIND STITCH

Come up at 1, go down at 2, and come up at 3 (**Fig. 37**). Length of stitches may be varied as desired.

Fig. 37

COUCHING STITCH

Come up at 1, go down at 2, and come up at 3. Continue until first stitch is evenly covered by small stitches (**Fig. 38**).

Fig. 38

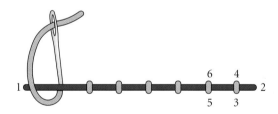

CROSS STITCH

Come up at 1 and go down at 2. Come up at 3 and go down at 4 (**Figs. 39 – 40**).

Fig. 39   **Fig. 40**

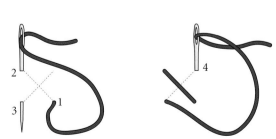

FRENCH KNOT

Follow **Figs. 41 – 44** to complete French Knots. Come up at 1. Wrap thread once around needle and insert needle at 2, holding end of thread with non-stitching fingers. Tighten knot, then pull needle through, holding floss until it must be released.

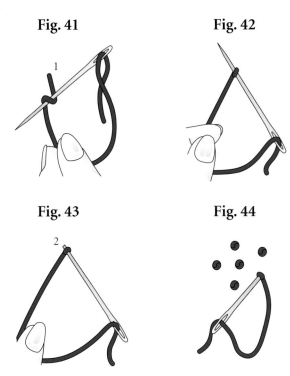

Fig. 41   **Fig. 42**

Fig. 43   **Fig. 44**

LAZY DAISY STITCH

Come up at 1 and go down again at 1 to form a loop. Come up at 2. Keeping loop below point of needle (**Fig. 45**), go down at 3 to anchor loop (**Fig. 46**).

Fig. 45   **Fig. 46**

RUNNING STITCH

The running stitch consists of a series of straight stitches with the stitch length equal to the space between stitches. Come up at 1, go down at 2, and come up at 3 (**Fig. 47**).

Fig. 47

SATIN STITCH

Come up at 1, go down at 2, and come up at 3. Continue until area is filled (**Fig.48**). Work stitches close together, but not overlapping.

Fig. 48

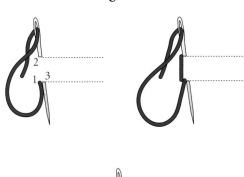

STEM STITCH

Come up at 1. Keeping thread below the stitching line, go down at 2 and come up at 3. Go down at 4 and come up at 5 (**Fig. 49**).

Fig. 49

STRAIGHT STITCH

Come up at 1 and go down at 2 (**Fig. 50**). Length of stitches may be varied as desired.

Fig. 50

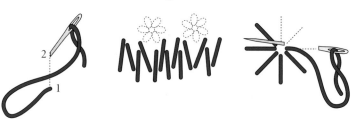

Metric Conversion Chart

Inches x 2.54 = centimeters (cm)	Yards x .9144 = meters (m)
Inches x 25.4 = millimeters (mm)	Yards x 91.44 = centimeters (cm)
Inches x .0254 = meters (m)	Centimeters x .3937 = inches (")
	Meters x 1.0936 = yards (yd)

Standard Equivalents

⅛"	3.2 mm	0.32 cm	⅛ yard	11.43 cm	0.11 m
¼"	6.35 mm	0.635 cm	¼ yard	22.86 cm	0.23 m
⅜"	9.5 mm	0.95 cm	⅜ yard	34.29 cm	0.34 m
½"	12.7 mm	1.27 cm	½ yard	45.72 cm	0.46 m
⅝"	15.9 mm	1.59 cm	⅝ yard	57.15 cm	0.57 m
¾"	19.1 mm	1.91 cm	¾ yard	68.58 cm	0.69 m
⅞"	22.2 mm	2.22 cm	⅞ yard	80 cm	0.8 m
1"	25.4 mm	2.54 cm	1 yard	91.44 cm	0.91 m